D0842693

Appreciation for the Work of
CHARLES T. TART

Open Mind, Discriminating Mind

"Fascinating. . . . [Tart] is the most important writer in the subject — the scientific study of expanded consciousness — in the world at the moment. The book I'm going to return to many times." — *Colin Wilson*

"A wonderful combination of discriminating science and open minded clarity, practicality, and humor." — *Roger Walsh, professor of psychiatry, University of California, Irvine, and author of* Staying Alive: The Psychology Of Survival

"The fascinating account of personal explorations in consciousness research by one of the world's leading experts in the field." — *Frances Vaughn, author of* Awakening Intuition *and* The Inward Arc

"Tart's research on the cutting edge of human consciousness demonstrates the psychological knowledge is far from complete, and filling in the gaps can be a scientific adventure." — *Stanley Krippner, professor of psychology, Saybrook Institute, and co-author of* Personal Mythology *and* Dream Working

Transpersonal Psychologies

"This fascinating book goes far beyond the promise of its title. It bridges the great yawning gap between the psychologies of the East and those of the West." — *J. B. Rhine*

"Many students of psychology and many patients undergoing psychotherapy complained that their professors and therapists ignore the spiritual dimensions of existence. Tart's magnificent book provides a corrective for this omission. This is a splendid volume!" — *Stanley Krippner*

Living The Mindful Life

"A practical and thoughtful users guide for applied mindfulness practice." — *Ram Dass*

"An excellent book of practical wisdom. It offers the reader an opportunity to actually practice exercises that were previously regarded as esoteric secrets." — *Frances Vaughan*

"Charles Tart is a pioneer in the integration of ancient wisdom and contemporary science. This book makes his many years of careful research and reflection available to us all."

— *Roger Walsh*

MIND SCIENCE

Meditation Training for Practical People

by

CHARLES T. TART, PH.D.

Institute of Transpersonal Psychology, Palo Alto
and
University of California at Davis

Wisdom Editions

NOVATO, CALIFORNIA

WISDOM EDITIONS
1122 Grant Avenue, Suite C
Novato, CA 94945
415-898-7400
www.ikosmos.com

Cover design by Phillip Dizick
Book design by Fearless Creative Services, Berkeley

Publisher's Cataloguing-in-Publication
(*Provided by Quality Books, Inc.*)

Tart, Charles T., 1937-
    Mind science : meditation training for
practical people / Charles T. Tart. — 1st ed.
    p. cm.
    LCCN: 00-108235
    ISBN: 1-931254-00-1

    1. Meditation. 2. Mind and body.   I. Title.

BF637.M4T37 2001   158.1'2
                    QBI00-500166

PRINTED IN THE UNITED STATES OF AMERICA ON RECYCLED PAPER

10 9 8 7 6 5 4 3 2 1

CONTENTS

ACKNOWLEDGEMENTS

This book would not have been possible without assistance from many people. Special thanks goes to my wife Judy for her support in so many ways and her detailed editorial help, as well as being a vital teacher to me.

Many people have acted as teachers and exemplars to me and so made this book, and what understanding I have, possible. As I do not know how to exactly weigh each teacher's contribution to this book, I will thank the more prominent ones here (under the socially acceptable convention of alphabetical order): James Baraz; Lama Anagarika Govinda; Arthur Hastings; Ernest Hilgard; Henry Korman; Jack Kornfield; Harold McCurdy; Claudio Naranjo; Jacob Needleman; Sogyal Rinpoche; Kathleen Riordan Speeth; Tarthang Tulku; Frances Vaughan; Roger Walsh; and Shinzen Young. I also want to thank my various Aikido teachers, who patiently and repeatedly forced me to learn the vital importance of body knowledge and body intelligence, usually by throwing me, lovingly but forcefully, across the dojo, until I got some understanding. Robert Frager inspired my wife and me to begin Aikido, and Alan Grow, Bruce Klickstein, Steve Sasaki and Pietro Maida trained us well.

DEDICATION

This book is dedicated to all those who suspect an important part of the answers to the questions and problems of life will come from becoming better acquainted with our internal, psychological functioning and by waking up from the dream-like fantasies that blind us from having and practicing insight and compassion.

Why Is A Scientist Writing a Book On Meditation And Mindfulness?

As we enter the twenty-first century, too many people are suffering. Much of this suffering is from factors way beyond my ability to affect, but a good deal of it is needless suffering that I can do a little about — suffering that stems from a widespread conflict between science and religion.

On the one hand, we have a science that apparently long ago showed that all religion and spirituality is superstitious and pathological nonsense left over from more primitive times, best thrown out as quickly and thoroughly as possible. On the other hand, we have both traditional religions and "New Age" spiritual movements appealing to something deep within us, but operating in a way often dissociated from scientific knowledge — or with thin and dubious rationalizations such as "Quantum physics is very mysterious, maybe religion is okay after all?" In between are we real human beings who *need* (psychologically as well as spiritually) a view of reality and our place in it that is much bigger and more meaningful than the apparently scientific, life-as-meaningless-biological-accident view associated with contemporary science, but who can't simply turn their backs on the great knowledge we've gained through science or deny its power.

Science gives us power, power to improve the world or destroy it, but gives us no moral guidance on using that power. Spirituality can give us compassion, morality and connectedness, but nineteenth and twentieth century science seems to have undermined spirituality, leaving us with increasing power but no clear morality. We cannot survive in this new millennium if this trend goes on.

I have struggled between these poles of conflict for many years and now reached a stage where I am comfortable with, indeed proud of, calling myself *both* a rigorous, no-nonsense *scientist* on the one hand and a *spiritual seeker* on the other.

The kind of resolution I've reached resulted in my teaching a 1998 workshop on how to practice meditation and mindfulness, as foundational keys to, among other things, *direct* psychological and, hopefully, spiritual experience about the mind instead of beliefs and dogmas about our nature. This workshop was for a group primarily composed of scholars and scientists at the University of Arizona's third "Toward a Science of Consciousness" meeting in Tucson. I believe the way I was able to successfully teach basic meditation and mindfulness practices for this audience is useful for all of us who've grown up in a culture that is dominated by science (and distorted ideas about what science is), whether we personally make our living as "scientists" or not. What we think of as scientific truths about the world have major effects on who and what we think we are and what is possible and impossible for us. This book is based on that workshop, deliberately keeping the informal style of a workshop but with the considerable improvement in phrasing that comes about with the wisdom of hindsight. My aim is to help others resolve the science versus spirituality conflict in at least some small way, so this new century can bring these two major forces together, not force them further apart.

This book is focused on giving the modern, Western reader, who is at least partially oriented toward scientific ways of thinking about things — that is, pretty much all of us — enough of a taste of basic methods of formal meditation practice and enhanced mindfulness in daily life to see what they are like and to see their advantages. There are suggestions for finding more advanced instruction and/or getting into the research literature, but this is not a scholarly book about meditation, nor a comprehensive review of the scientific research that has been done on it.

Nor is this a book about religion — but Western religion has affected all of us strongly, whether we consciously accept it or reject it, so let's talk more about religion.

Like many of us, I was raised with strong Western religious beliefs — Missouri Synod Lutheran in my case — and, as a child, I basically believed what I was taught. The universe was created by God and existed for His Reasons. Our job (a tough, if not impossible one!) was to avoid sin and be good — or else! But at least life made a kind of sense and the rules were clear.

By the time I was a teenager, reading a lot and thinking for myself, problems arose with this simple faith. I wanted to be "good," but interpretation of exactly what was good and bad got quite difficult at times, and the behavior of many adults I knew, who professed to be religious, often seemed inconsistent and hypocritical.

I also became more and more fascinated by science, reading voraciously, and the conflict between science and religion became very real for me — as happens for so many of us in modern Western culture. While some scientists of the past saw their work as revealing the glories of God ever more deeply, most scientists today apparently have no use for God or Divine Plans in a scientific world view, and many have claimed and continue to claim that *all* of religion is primitive, superstitious nonsense that we should leave behind, indeed that religions have vastly increased craziness and suffering in the world. As I now could recognize many examples of pathology in common religious doctrines, practices and ideas, this was a powerful argument.

And yet . . . was religion *totally* nonsense? Or was there some core of valuable truth hidden down among doctrines, theologies, rituals and customs? I struggled a lot with these kinds of questions in my teenage years.

Many of my contemporaries went through similar struggles, and I suspect many of you have also. As an adult, with the wisdom of hindsight, I was able to see the most common kinds of apparent resolutions people found. One common pattern was for people to become materialists and thus reject religion entirely, as indeed being nothing but total nonsense. This pattern of resolution varied from simple agnosticism at the one extreme to a strong denial of God's existence in those who became passionate, atheistic materialists. In some of my friends this kind of passion was a reactive anger to disappointment in practicing their childhood religion, a kind of "If God won't answer my prayers (the way I want them answered) I won't believe in him!" response, later rationalized as a logical decision to reject religion for lack of evidence.

Another common pattern was one that, as a psychologist, I can retrospectively call mild dissociation or *compartmentalization*. Religion was put into a mental compartment that was only opened for a few hours on Saturday or Sunday, and that compartment was kept shut the rest of the week so as to not interfere with materialistic, secular life.

Sound familiar?

I was lucky to find a third way which, again with the wisdom of hindsight, I think is a healthier one that involves neither totally ignoring religion nor reactive anger nor the fragmentation of wholeness that's involved in any kind of dissociative coping strategy. In my extensive reading in many fields of science, in religion, metaphysics, psychology, philosophy and parapsychology, I slowly learned three crucial distinctions, which might be expressed as follows:

Science ≠ Scientism

Spirituality ≠ Religion

Belief ≠ Direct Experience

Science ≠ Scientism

With respect to science, I discovered that because it's such a valued activity with high social prestige, practically everybody wants to be considered scientific. So we have many outspoken people denying or attacking religion who claim that they are being scientific, but these claims often mask simple human beliefs, arrogance and prejudice that cause people to take quite unscientific positions — something we will occasionally look at in detail in this book. When current scientific theories about the physical world that work well (even if not perfectly) undergo a psychological shift to The Truth, are held with arrogance, and are used as a rationale to attack facts and beliefs that don't correspond with them, we effectively have a dogmatic religion made of current scientific theories, *scientism*. This distinction between science and scientism, as sociologists took to calling it back in the 40s (see, e.g., (Bannister 1987) (Schoek and Wiggins 1960) (Wellmuth 1944)), is very important.

Spirituality ≠ Religion

With respect to religion, I discovered that there are what we might call *primary spiritual experiences*, which are the mainsprings powering religion. Religion is a social development that usually started with important, alive, personal spiritual experiences by the founders of the religion. But, too often, the ideas and injunctions supposedly rooted in those experiences have gotten so far from the original spiritual experiences, and gotten so altered by ordinary social and personal needs, as to become a very distorted and pathological system indeed. It's a long way, for example, from Jesus' injunction to love one another to the all-too-common "Kill the heathens!" attitude that has too often manifested in our culture.

These two discoveries, that science is not the same as scientism and that spirituality is not the same as religion, are hardly unique to me, of course, but since *my* struggle was affecting *me*, the personal understanding of these was important to me. Because my struggle between science and religion was similar to that of so many of us today, these distinctions are important to us all.

There is a genuine scientific enterprise, carried out in accordance with the goals and principles of what I like to call *essential science*, which is discussed in this book, leading to working hypotheses, tentative conclusions, always subject to further test against data, including the data of experience. There is genuine spiritual inquiry which, carried out with humility, a quality usually deemed essential to spiritual development, also leads to working hypotheses, tentative conclusions, *always* subject to further test against data, including the data of experience. I find these two activities compatible in principle — and as I mentioned above, I can say that I'm comfortable calling myself both a rigorous scientist and a spiritual seeker.

Then there is the "religion" of scientism versus traditional religion, which will always have many conflicts with each other, conflicts often motivated on both sides by fear and anger, insecurity and reaction to childhood disappointments. In both cases what should be *tentative working hypotheses/ beliefs*, the best we can do for the time being but subject, with humility, to further test, become Truths which are defended against perceived Heresy. When people are psychologically and illogically emotionally attached to their beliefs, they will always be threatened by others who don't share them.

Belief ≠ Direct Experience

Now, why am I saying so much about religion, spirituality and science in a book that focuses on meditation and mindfulness? This brings us to the third distinction I slowly learned, that belief is not the same as direct experience. Our Western religions are generally quite authoritarian. "This is the Truth! Believe it and live by the Rules, or go to Hell! If you doubt, if you question, that's a sin!" Quite aside from all the nasty psychological consequences this attitude brings about when it's forced on children or adults, it's completely incompatible with the basic scientific attitude. This scientific attitude assumes we're pretty ignorant about the nature of reality, but that we can find out more and more about all of reality through disciplined investigation. It's an attitude that wants to find out.

Meditation and mindfulness practices, our focus in this book, are not doctrines or religious "truths," except in the very minor sense that it's believed that becoming more mindful will lead to better outcomes in life than being insensitive and ignorant. I think that's an essential working belief if we are to move on from where we are: after all, if we believe mindfulness won't help us we won't try it and, sure enough, it won't help us — which doesn't tell us anything. Meditation and mindfulness practices are *methods* for discovering fundamental truths about yourself and about reality *for yourself.* Methods for getting more direct knowledge, *data*, instead of being satisfied with beliefs and theories given you by authorities. Methods that you have to *practice* and see what happens, not beliefs to hold or reject.

Although there have been Western meditation and mindfulness methods, as rather esoteric parts of Judaism and Christianity, we had pretty much lost meditation and mindfulness practices as a culture until the infusion of workable methods from Eastern cultures, starting in the 60s and continuing through today. This is not to say, of course, that

Easterners can't be as stuck and blinded in religious beliefs as we can. I have been a student (not the best student, by any means, but a pretty serious one) of Eastern spiritual meditation and mindfulness methods for several decades. While I still primarily see myself as a scientist, and certainly not an accomplished meditator or a "mystic," I have learned enough to be able to teach the basic methods in ways that work for modern Westerners, especially the scientifically trained and inclined. And, given the pervasiveness of science throughout modern, global culture, *we are all scientifically inclined, whether we consciously know it or not.* So this book is intended to be helpful to everyone, not just those who are socially identified as scientists.

If you are personally curious about yourself, the world, life, if you would like to see us develop a better scientific understanding of the mind, of consciousness, then I think you will find this book not only intellectually stimulating, but practically useful. Put aside, for now, the religious beliefs that may have been forced on you as a child, that you may still actively hold or react against, or may hold in that special Sabbath compartment. Put aside, for now, the scientistic and materialistic doctrines that automatically deny any reality to your spiritual side, whatever that may be. Try collecting your own data by learning and practicing the basic meditation and mindfulness practices presented here, and see for yourself what it's all about.

As mentioned above, this book is the outcome of a pre-conference workshop on meditation and mindfulness practice that I gave in April 1998 at the University of Arizona's third "Toward A Science of Consciousness" conference. Giving this workshop was an interesting experiment for me. My students were almost exclusively working scientists, or people with a strong enough interest in the scientific study of consciousness to travel to Arizona and pay for a five-day conference on scientific, scholarly and philosophical attempts to understand consciousness.

I have something of an ironic sense of humor, and I originally thought of calling the workshop "Meditation and Mindfulness for the Scientifically Handicapped," as I am very aware from my own experience and work with others that science can so easily turn into the corrosive, unhealthy pseudo-skepticism of scientism. Scientists may have an especially hard time getting beyond these habits. As I reflected, though, and with good advice from my wife Judy, I realized this was a poor, if humorous, title. Perhaps a compromise, "Meditation and Mindfulness for the Scientifically Talented/Handicapped"? After all, the training in disciplined thinking and action, and the innate curiosity that draws most scientists to such a profession in the first place, are definite advantages. I ended up with "Observing the Mind: Basic Training in Skilled Means," which was perfect for Tucson III, as many people studying the mind are beginning to recognize that getting a really scientific understanding is not a simple matter of better data than just anyone noticing what goes on in their own mind and thinking they have observed the Real Phenomena of General Mind. It will indeed require more skillful ways of observing the mind than we ordinarily have, and "skillful means" is a classical description of meditation practices.

The workshop was a great success, both from my view as the teacher and from the reports of the 40+ students. The scientifically inclined — practically all of us Westerners — do indeed have talents for this kind of learning, as well as blocks. I have kept the informal workshop style in this book, as so many people prefer that, but have added clarifications and information on resources.

Don't be discouraged if initially learning meditation and mindfulness in life is hard for you. It's easy for some people, but it was especially hard for me, with an overly active, overly skeptical mind, yet I eventually learned enough that meditation and mindfulness are some of the most valued parts of my life. If you learn these basic meditation and mindfulness techniques, perhaps you'll become a better scientist. Perhaps you'll become a better person. Perhaps you'll have some spiritual experiences — perhaps you won't. Perhaps you'll just become more practical, intelligent and sensitive through a clearer perception of what actually goes on in your own mind and in the world. That's mainly what's happened to me, but that's me, not you. And perhaps . . . who knows what you might learn as you become a more skilled observer of your own mind and self?

But you won't know unless you give it a good try! Modern science arose as a reaction to the authoritarian attitudes of the Church, which said that if you wanted to know Truth, just read the accepted Scriptures, believe what the approved authorities said. Science claimed the right to go out and actually look at data! The authorities said that the heavier a body was, the faster it fell. Science went out and looked at actual falling bodies and discovered that, once you ruled out air friction in light objects, all bodies fell at the same rate.

We have a lot of opinions, received truths about the mind from authority figures, many of them conditioned into us when we were children but still operating today. The skilled means of meditation and mindfulness in life give us a chance to find out what's really there for ourselves, and quite "ordinary" people can go a long way — if they learn and try.

As Henry Ford is supposed to have said, "Those who think they can and those who think they can't are both right."

Institute of Transpersonal Psychology
Palo Alto, California
July, 2000

The Tucson III Workshop

Good morning!
This is the workshop on meditation and awareness for the scientifically inclined. Here is the "official" description of what we're about today:

The Consciousness Studies Program
at the University of Arizona
Presents
Tucson III: Toward A Science of Consciousness 1998
Pre-Conference Workshop
On
Observing the Mind: Basic Training in Skilled Means
With
Dr. Charles Tart

In the last century, psychologists tried to develop a science of the mind using introspective data and failed.

A major reason for this failure is that the ordinary mind has little skill at observing itself. The "normal" state of consensus consciousness is like a virtual reality, generating apparently real experiences based on cultural conditioning and often distorting perception to support these scenarios. This workshop will introduce participants to three basic techniques for calming the mind (concentrative meditation), developing deeper understanding of the mind (insight meditation), and becoming able to observe deeper mental processes under ordinary life conditions (Gurdjieffian self-remembering). The emphasis is on learning actual skills. These skills can make us better scientists, improve our ability to obtain actual data about consciousness, and apply to personal efforts such as stress reduction, and clearer reality contact. Prior reading of Tart's books *Waking Up* and *Living the Mindful Life* would be helpful, but is not required.

So if you're in the wrong workshop, you're not very mindful and you've flunked this course already, without even having had to try anything!

Just kidding! I know that I tripped over the rug coming up onto this platform a minute ago, so everybody who saw that has good reason not to acquire any delusions about how aware I actually am.

Mindfulness is wonderful stuff to think about. I can recall riding in my carpool up to UC Davis once. I had some wonderful ideas about the nature of mindfulness, made some notes on my laptop and, as I got out of the van, I was telling some people about these wonderful insights into mindfulness I'd had. And I tripped over one of the concrete barriers in the parking lot — I wasn't paying attention to what I was actually doing!

That's a funny anecdote, but it presents one of the most important things that I'll have to keep coming back to over and over and over again. *Thoughts about being more mindful are not the same as actually being more mindful!*

Now due to the nature of our society today, I imagine — either sometimes because of personal involvement or to be supportive to a friend — everybody here has been to an Alcoholics Anonymous meeting or knows about AA meetings. So I thought I would start this workshop by introducing myself in AA style.

Hi! My name is Charley and *thoughts* are my drug of abuse. Thoughts get me high! I love them and I can't get enough of them! Some kinds of thoughts are better than others, like abstract concepts, and especially *theories*! Oh boy, I can really get high on theories!

We very much live in a world of thought, which is good in a lot of ways — except that we're really carried away by thoughts too much of the time. One of the consequences of this being carried away is that it impairs our reality contact. We *think* we're in touch with what's going around us and with ourselves, but much of the time when we think that, we're actually significantly lost in concepts and beliefs, in hopes and fears about what's going on, concepts and beliefs and hopes and fears about both outside events and inside events. As a consequence, we generate consequences, what Easterners would call *karma*, or to put it in more straightforward terms, we do stupid things: if you don't really know what's going on around you, the actions you take, based on distorted conceptions, based on living in your head instead of in reality, lead to trouble.

I've worded the description of today's workshop differently than I usually do. I occasionally lead workshops on meditation, or on increased awareness in everyday life, and the people who come are primarily people who are interested in some kind of spiritual development, or in some kind of psychological self-improvement. That may be true today but the official "Toward A Science of Consciousness — Tucson III" description we're here under is that we're people interested in the scholarly and scientific study of consciousness, so we're all scientists and scholars. An implication that we're a "higher" class of people than just ordinary folks. Yes?

(Affirmative and amused responses from workshop participants)

Okay, that's what I wanted to hear. Now I'm going to work within that "fiction," partially because it's true, and also because, as a result of my own work over the years, I've come to see that being both a good scientist and being someone interested in spiritual psychological growth are quite compatible. There is not an inherent conflict between the two as many people seem to think. Indeed they can be synergistic — and that's the basis I'm going to work from today.

I'm going to give you some background first — the "why to" — and then we're going to spend a good deal of our time together practicing various kinds of techniques, the "how to." There will be a lot of emphasis on techniques, because I don't want to give you just some more "high proof ideas" for you to get intellectually drunk on. I want to give you some actual practices you can take home with you, work with to develop your own mindfulness abilities, and begin to get a little direct knowledge of what is being talked about when we talk about mindfulness.

CHAPTER 1

Science and Meditation
Are Compatible

Essential Science versus Scientism

The background framework I want to remind you about is what I call essential science, which I will end up distinguishing from what most people mistakenly think science is, which tends to be *scientism*.

Essential science is basically a four-stage process. It starts out with curiosity about the world, about yourself, about any particular subject you're interested in, combined with a certain amount of humility. It's curiosity plus the fact that you realize there are a lot of things you don't know that you'd like to know.

If you think you know everything about the area you're interested in, then you're not into investigating anything. You may be into trying to convince other people of the rightness of your position, to cram your "truth" down reluctant throats, or something like that, and while it may look externally like what many people think is science, it's not real science. So essential science starts out with curiosity and humility.

Getting the Data

Given that recognition and the motivation to learn, the first and most important step in the process of essential science is getting the *data*. Go out there and observe what actually goes on. If it's an area in the "external world," outside immediate "internal" experience, observe it. If you're interested in some aspect of botany, for example, don't just think about it, go out and look at the plants. If you're interested in the way your mind works, instead of just thinking about it, try to somehow develop a way to observe how your mind actually works.

In all of these cases, because you have a certain amount of humility, you go out and get the data but you also realize, "I'm probably not the world's best observer. It may be I don't look at things very carefully. I might even be biased about some things." This must be a personal understanding, not just a concept. My wife, for example, tells me I'm a terrible observer. She is absolutely amazed at how I can get by in science when I can't find things in the house when she says they are right in front of me. Okay, but I don't claim to be a good observer in all areas of life! So you have or develop some understanding that you're not the world's best observer: how can you improve your ability to get better data, to see what's really going on?

In the physical sciences, this question is usually answered by working to invent instruments for seeing things more clearly. So you invent a magnifying glass, for example, and suddenly you can see fine aspects of the structure of plants which you couldn't have seen with your naked eye. For a psychological parallel let's say you're interested in the psychology of aggression when people are in bars. After trying to make observations for a while, you realize that sometimes things happen too fast and/or complexly for you to observe what's going on very clearly, so maybe you have to set up and train a team of observers, each of whom is only looking at one aspect of the action. Then each one can observe that one part much more clearly without getting distracted by the rest of the action. You put these various observations from your "instrument" together and you can learn something.

If you're interested in the psychology of your own mind, maybe you can develop some kind of instrument that gives you clearer access to the data of your own mind. That's a major part of our work together today.

The main techniques I'm going to teach you today — which we will call (a) *concentrative meditation*, (b) *insight/opening up/vipassana meditation*, and (c) *self-remembering/self-observation* in everyday life — are three major techniques to enable you to get a clearer idea of what's going on in your own mind.

Theorizing

Okay, you find ways of getting the data, you try to see as much as possible about whatever part of the world you're interested in, take good notes on it rather than depending on your memory, somehow systematize what you've seen, and you've got data. That's the most important part of the essential aspect of science, but science doesn't stop there because, by and large, we don't care that much about what the data is. We want to know what the data means. *Why* does this plant grow in this particular fashion, not the way its neighboring plants grow? *Why* do I get agitated in certain kinds of situations and my neighbor hardly even notices them, she stays so calm? *Why* does my mind go off in this kind of emotional loop when other people's minds don't seem to react in the same way to the same situation?

So the second step in essential science is to *theorize*, to try to figure out the underlying reasons the data turns out the way it does, the causes behind the phenomena. The basic rule is to try to theorize *logically*. (Or to express the theory logically in its final form, no matter what mental processes got you there.) It turns out there are lots of different logics, of course, but if you're going to pick a logic (differential calculus, for example) you use it consistently, follow its rules, and so you theorize logically about your data. You do that until the moment of "Aha!" comes, the moment when you say "Aha! That's why things are that way!"

The experience of insight and discovery is a wonderful moment in life! It's one of the most satisfying things in existence when you figure out why things happen the way they do. That's also why I'm a thoughtaholic. I love that moment of insight!

Now both essential science and real psychological and spiritual growth add a vital discipline requirement at this point. They both have a recognition of what I like to call the *universal principle of rationalization.* In retrospect, you can take any set in the world of observations, of facts, of experiences and come up with some idea that seems to fit them together plausibly, even if they are not connected in reality. We are all world class rationalizers. We can always connect things in some way that seems plausible. And that's very satisfying, but the discipline is to recognize that your wonderful theory, which may be mathematical, elegant and logical, which may incorporate all the currently popular buzzwords — "Oh, I observed that data because of quantum fluctuations in the chaotic tensor fields of the morphogenetic resonance vectors" — may not be right. It may have all the things that make it a socially acceptable, really hot sounding theory, but that is not sufficient. It could be (as you learn in retrospect) a rationalization; I emphasize again, you can always come up with some intellectual framework that makes apparent sense of something.

Testing, Testing, Testing

Constantly remembering that theory is always secondary to, always to be judged by data, is a vital discipline in science and should be a vital discipline in spiritual and psychological growth — but often it is not, in both areas. So when confronted by a wonderful set of ideas, a wonderful theory, you say, "Okay, here's my great sounding theory, here's my logic that puts everything together. Fine! Continue to work with logic and make predictions about things I haven't observed. Then go out back into where I gather my experience, my data, and test to see if the predictions come true."

For example, I postulate a universal theory of gravitation whereby every material object will be drawn toward any other object, and I make a prediction that when I let go of this particular cassette tape box, which I've never dropped before, it will fall. *(CTT drops tape box, it falls.)* Ah, once again my theory works!

I've been waiting for the day this example fails! That's going to be quite exciting, but so far that old theory of universal gravitation has been very reliable.

We have some theories that work very well. They predict things in a lot of situations. This example was a specific, new prediction. Nobody's ever dropped this particular tape box in this particular room. On the other hand, it's pretty trivial, we're so used to that kind of thing working. But this is the discipline that is essential in science. It says no matter how satisfied you are with your theory, no matter how much you feel you know the Truth, no matter how elegant it is, you've got to make predictions about new things you haven't observed yet *and go out and test them.* See if it works. If it does predict correctly, good, you'll feel very satisfied. If it doesn't work, your theory is in trouble. It doesn't matter how obviously true it is, if your theory says "If A, then B," and you set up A and B doesn't happen, your theory's in trouble.

Now maybe sometimes a minor modification of the theory

will do the trick, but maybe sometimes no modification of the theory, no working within that framework of belief and logic will do anything to reconcile prediction and observation, and you've got to come up with a whole new theory. It's back to the basic data, to come up with some whole new ways of thinking about them.

The Social Dimension of Science: Consensual Validation

As I've described the process of science so far, it can be done by a solitary individual. I've said this basic observation-theory-prediction/testing cycle should happen within the spiritual disciplines and the psychological growth disciplines too, as well as in essential science, but its not clear that it always does. Again that deep intellectual and emotional satisfaction of "Ah! I've figured it all out!" is so satisfying it can stop further mental activity, whether that figuring it out has been some kind of reasoning process applied to the data of the external world or of your own experience, or whether it's a result of some mystical experience, some altered state experience, where the light has suddenly struck and now you know that you understand everything. The fact that we're human, whether we're functioning as a scientist or non-scientist, means we really do tend to stop at that point of satisfying "understanding."

Then, of course, we get emotionally attached to our wonderful insight. We don't want it to be wrong or trivial, and so we may end up constricting our life so we don't run into any situations where our theory might not pass the test of making correct predictions. We fall in love with our theories. So, for example, let's say you have a "mystical experience" and *know*, deep in your heart, that, say, Love is the only real force in the universe. Now you walk up to a stranger on the street and enthusiastically say, "Love is everything!" She slaps your face and walks away. Well, at the very least, the theory needs some modifications, Okay, love may be important but there are some adjustments needed, some other factors that need to be brought in. And maybe the theory is wrong no matter how appealing or "obviously" true it is.

In spiritual traditions such as Buddhism, the problem with our falling in love with our theories would be referred to by the technical term attachment. You get attached to a particular concept, a particular set of beliefs, a particular emotional experience — and, from the perspective of the psychology of Buddhism, all attachment leads to trouble. It doesn't matter if it's attachment to a wonderful idea versus a sickening idea, attachment leads to trouble.

Okay, so science as I've described it, spiritual growth as I've described it, can be done on the individual level. This is what one person can do and it's done as a continual, cyclical process. You start out really ignorant but curious, you make some observations, you come up with some ideas that make some sense of the observations, you test them. Some of the predictions work, some of them don't, so then you go back to the data. Then you come up with a better theory that makes more correct predictions, etc. As time goes on you gradually make better and better observations of whatever it is you're interested in and you come up with better and better ideas/theories to put it together. This is one-person science or one-person growth.

The problem with this is that each one of us is undoubtedly strangely and uniquely flawed or biased in ways that are almost impossible for us to see ourselves. To compensate, science becomes a social enterprise and spiritual growth may become a social enterprise. You add an essential fourth step to these three other steps of data-theory-prediction, namely the step of full communication with your peers. We can define your "peers" as being people you think know something about your area of interest, people whose opinions you have respect for.

So when you observe things, you tell other people, your peers, *exactly* what you observed. They can then go out and take a look. They might then say, "I went out and did that experiment or went to that place or did that meditation technique and I didn't notice that thing you reported to me at all." Hmm! Well, maybe there is something else you need to specify in order for others to be able to observe what you reported. Or maybe your or others' observations were flawed; there was some kind of shortcoming or bias.

Or someone else might say, "I observed those things you reported as data with my new super-duper instruments, and I can give you a more precise report of exactly what it was you observed." So by adding the communication process to observation, other people expand your own observations, your own experiences, and act as a brake on possible biases you may have. The same thing can happen when you do your theorizing, when you explain the logic of your theory to other people. Someone else may then say, "Well that was pretty good at first, but then in this equation you said 2 + 2 = 3. Since you said you were using the logic of ordinary arithmetic, that does not compute." So other people may catch your errors in the logic of your theory, and/or they may say, "Ah! Very good. Now I can add a chaos theory perspective to this particular thing and it explains more." Your theory now has a whole new dimension added to it.

For spiritual growth, we also come up with theories and understandings based on our experiences/observations, so we can have the same social dimension with the requirement to go out and test your predictions that are based on your understanding. Other people can test your theory's implications/predictions in different, more extensive ways than you can, other people can communicate back to you and come up with other confirmations you might not have thought about. So you get a decided social advantage in that your individual abilities are both multiplied and checked by the abilities of many.

So science and spiritual growth become a social process. Instead of just you alone doing your best, but perhaps being seriously blocked by biases and distortions you don't even know you have, other people try it in a variety of ways and that helps compensate for what your particular shortcomings might be. In the case of spiritual growth, for instance, you may learn some meditation technique, practice it for a while and have some wonderful experiences. Lets take a classical teaching story from Zen Buddhism.

A student had been practicing for several years with a meditation technique of single-minded concentration on the breath. While practicing one day, he was suddenly transported to the heaven realms! Gods and goddesses appeared and bowed down to him, flowers rained from the air and sweet scents wafted by, and he knew he was Blessed and Chosen! After he came out of it, he ran up to the Zen master and breathlessly told the Zen master about it! As he was waxing on rhapsodically, though, the Zen master interrupted and said, "Excuse me, were you aware of your breathing all of this time? . . . No? Go back and practice more, remember to keep your focus on your breath."

Please be clear that I am not devaluing unusual, "spiritual" experiences in general here by recounting this teaching story. Such experiences, in other contexts, can be vital growth steps for a person, and my TASTE web site[1] is intended to respect and facilitate the sharing of such experiences. But within the context of trying to learn to concentrate, distraction is distraction, even if it seems wonderful.

Other people can act as a way of keeping you focused, as a check that you're following directions. Whether that check is in the direction of freedom-depriving mind control, to just briefly introduce a dimension we will come back to later, or whether it's in the direction of clearly increasing the full range of your knowledge — well, that an interesting and vital question! In a spiritual discipline, a teacher may indeed help you keep widening your horizons — in Zen, rapturous experiences with gods and goddesses are seen as a diversion that can turn into a serious trap, keeping the student from real enlightenment — or, on the negative side, may subtly, and sometimes not so subtly, narrow your experience so that you stop growing.

Okay, I've given you an introduction to the essential science background I'm bringing to our work today. Essential science is to get out there and see what happens, observe, get the facts, get the data whether it's outside stuff or your own or others' experience. Then you go and figure out what that's all about, theorize, try to be logical about your thinking, and keep it up until you feel you understand. Once you understand, don't be satisfied with that "Aha!" feeling, though; test the consequences of the logic of your theory. If they don't work, come up with a new theory, and if they do work, fine! Keep working with it and refine it.

Now there is an interesting psychological event that happens that's particularly important to understand with a scientifically oriented group like this. Sometimes, within science, we get a theory that is really, really good, a super theory. One theory, one new way of understanding things, suddenly makes so much sense out of almost everything considered important in the field that people now forget that the essence of science is that the data is *always* what's most important, that theories are important but *always* subject to test. Instead they implicitly feel that they now know the *Truth*.

Here, I'll drop this tape cassette box again. Okay, why does this fall? I'm sure the words that automatically come to a lot of people's minds is it fell because of the operation of the Law of Gravity, with a capital L on that "law." When a super theory comes along, when the *paradigm*, as Thomas Kuhn (Kuhn 1962) called it, comes along, we make a subtle but very important psychological step where we forget that facts, data, experience, are primary, and instead we now become kind of arrogant. We are so smart, we figured out these fundamental laws of the universe!

Now a paradigm does a lot of good for a field of science in many ways. A theory that obviously works very well tends to then tightly focus scientists' efforts in that field, so they can investigate phenomena in immense detail, which frequently also leads to great progress. Kuhn called the stage after a paradigm developed for a field, leading to scientific activity within the guiding framework of the paradigm, *normal science*. The paradigm explicitly and implicitly focuses people on "significant" problems in the field to refine, rather than having their efforts be scattered.

The negative side of paradigmatic science comes, first, from the attitude of arrogance, whether that attitude is conscious and explicit or unconscious and implicit. Taking that attitude of knowing Truth, I now implicitly or explicitly think, "Since I understand everything important about (my part of) Reality, if you mention anything to me that doesn't obviously make sense within my paradigm, you're either ignorant or some kind of fool, and I don't have to waste my time listening to you." The paradigmatic attitude is not quite that obvious most of the time but that's the effect it has. It narrows people's openness to look at all aspects of reality. The fact that people making claims that don't make sense within the paradigm sometimes turn out to be ignorant or fools reinforces this attitude that we already know everything important and anyone who makes claims that don't fit the paradigm *must* be mistaken or a fool.

The second problem is that the paradigm narrows your perception because it's been so successful. It defines what's important to investigate further and what's not important, what's "trivial" and may be ignored. It defines certain problems, and getting finer and finer solutions of them (within the paradigm) becomes the core work of the discipline, and it makes other things trivial or nominally of no importance whatsoever. That, coupled with the tendency to automatic arrogance, essentially means a paradigm is a tremendously narrow focusing. You've got a telescope or a microscope, as it were. Within those instruments' fields you see very, very well, but you tend not to see things outside their fields of view at all. If people mention things outside those fields, you tend to pity these poor fools that don't have a nice microscope or telescope like you, who don't know anything.

Okay, we are all members of fields of knowledge dominated by various paradigms. We are all immersed in many paradigms, both interlocking and unrelated, simply by being members of Western culture, not to mention any specific scientific discipline we've been trained in. And by and large, we don't know we have them: paradigms tend to become unconscious.

When I took physics in high school and college, no one taught me about the *theory* of gravity, but that's really what the so-called Law of Gravity actually is. The idea that masses have an inherent attraction for each other, that is a theory. It makes excellent sense out of enormous masses of data, but it's a theory and, in principle, it's subject to more tests. But nobody ever taught me that. They taught me about the Law of Gravity, and obviously you can't have any exceptions to the Law.

We have paradigms in the sense of habits of thinking, ways in which our mind automatically focuses in certain directions under certain circumstances and, by and large, these habits, these implicit paradigms, come to seem "natural." We don't even know we have these habits. That's just the "natural" way to think.

Early Psychology as a Science of Mind

Our presence at this "Toward A Science of Consciousness" conference indicates that we want a science of mind. When psychology started out as a new field in the last century, it was going to be a science of mind. It was going to follow the rules of essential science. We would get some trained observers who would observe certain aspects of the way the mind functions and report on them, thus generating our data. We would then come up with theories to explain these observations, go on to test and refine the theories and so forth, following the process of essential science.

What happened? This attempt failed miserably. We ended up having prominent laboratories, many in Germany, who had their trained introspectives, their observers, who would say, "The taste of chocolate is smooth," and another laboratory whose introspectives would say that the taste of chocolate is obviously bumpy. (These are not actual examples, just the kind of thing that happened.)

Now, it's hard to develop any science if people can't agree on the basic data. If you can't start out with clear and reliable observations of what's out there, your theorizing about it doesn't make all that much sense. Introspective psychology, our first modern attempt to create a science of mind, failed, and was replaced by rigid Behaviorism, which essentially decreed, "Ignore everything that goes on inside the mind and we'll look only at how people behave. Observations of behavior are reliable but reports of experience are not, so we can build a science of behavior. But introspection is hopeless."

Observing behavior is indeed far more reliable than trying to observe experience: you can get a hundred percent agreement on whether or not I lift up this tape box and put it down at this time, but probably far less than a hundred percent agreement on what I really meant to illustrate by doing that. Studying behavior has been really useful, there is no doubt about that. But when you say studying behavior is the *only* thing you can possibly be scientific about and come up with a worthwhile psychology about, that's silly. You've thrown out too many of the most interesting things in life.

So what happened with the early introspectionists? Why did this first attempt at a Western science of consciousness fail?

I am aware of several problems when I look back on that

history. For one thing, they believed they were having introspection done on various phenomena by trained observers. What was a *trained* observer? Someone who had received 10-20 hours of practice in how to observe some particular phenomenon. Are they really "trained"?

If you look from the perspective of an Eastern psychological tradition, Buddhism, where people work on observing the mind with techniques that we're going to start talking about and practicing in a few minutes, they were not. The general guideline I've gotten from several experienced teachers of Buddhist meditation practice is that after perhaps 5,000 hours of basic meditation training, a person is getting into a position to actually begin to observe something worthwhile, instead of being caught up in their own delusions! Our early introspectionist observers really had no clear idea how to observe their minds; they were totally untrained by Buddhist standards.

Let me use another analogy to bring that point home, too. This is a Hindu analogy, which says that in the depths of our minds are great treasures — but there is a problem in getting them. Our minds are like a lake on which a storm is blowing. The waters are constantly agitated. When you try to look through the surface of the lake to see the treasures in the depths, you generally can't see them, or you may sometimes get a momentary, but generally distorted, glimpse of them because of the agitation of the water. What you think is here is actually over there, size and shape are distorted, etc. No way are you going to clearly see the treasures in the depths until you learn to still the waves by calming the storm. Until you learn to still that incredible agitation that is ordinary consciousness, agitation that is so habitual you hardly even notice it, you can forget about observing the really worthwhile stuff, the treasures that are inside your mind.

So there was one major failing of introspective psychology. They had no idea how much training it took, nor how to train people to begin to allow a new kind of depth observation of our own minds to be possible.

Secondly, there was a major problem of bias. I mentioned a few minutes ago that having a spiritual mentor can be a very helpful communication process, like the full and honest communications process in essential science, that may help you to expand your horizons as you discover things about your own mind, or that it may act as a form of thought control, as a form of "Forget that experience, concentrate on this experience because it is doctrinally correct," or something like that. We had a similar bias problem in earlier introspective psychology. Remember much of it was done in Germany, a highly authoritarian culture at the time. The introspectors were laboratory assistants working for Herr Doctor Professor Great Man, who had his own theories about what should be observed. To say that bias might have been communicated at times as to what they were supposed to see, is probably to put it mildly.

So, we have two essential elements to think about then if we're going to establish a science of consciousness *per se*. I don't mean some other field that then explains consciousness *away*, but a science of consciousness *per se*, where direct, interior observation of consciousness is the primary field of data. The first is that we've got to cut down the agitation of ordinary, everyday consciousness so that we have a chance of seeing past the surface of the lake, and the second is that we have to be very careful of creating biases, or not recognizing already existing biases, that are going to distort what it is we manage to see.

Okay, we've had too much theory for a workshop that intends to emphasize experiential work, but I warned you, I'm a thoughtaholic! But I'm sure I'm not the only thoughtaholic in the room, so it's been important to establish a basis for scientifically oriented people to find it legitimate and sensible to work with meditation and mindfulness. I can't help getting conceptual at times, and I will undoubtedly share more conceptual material with you off and on all through the day, but let's actually begin now with some practice.

CHAPTER 2

Concentrative Meditation

I'm assuming most of you are relatively new or totally new to something like meditation. If you're a really advanced meditator you're going to be disappointed in me!

It's funny, when the Tucson III conference program came out, one of my meditation teachers, who I think is one of the best meditation teachers in the world, called me up, and said "I saw you will be giving a workshop on meditation and mindfulness." This is Shinzen Young, who I will recommend anytime as a meditation teacher. I thought "Oh boy! The real teacher has caught me faking it!" So I told him "Well look, you know, when you're around, I'm just a student, but for the man in the street, I am a pretty good meditation teacher."

In fact, actually I'm an especially good meditation teacher for novices when it comes to the *difficulties* of learning meditation, because I've experienced them all, but no one would ever call me a really good or talented meditator. I've struggled at length to get the little bit of knowledge of meditation that

I have, so I can say things about the difficulties that people experience that may be meaningful.

All right, let's move on then. I'm going to teach three major techniques today. One of them is *concentrative meditation*. This is the basic quieting and focusing exercise. This is the one to cut down that raging mental storm so you start to have a chance of looking at what's underneath the surface of ordinary consciousness. In scientific terms, it's cleaning the instrument, as it were, so you have a chance at making useful observations instead of just looking at all the dust on your microscope lens. Concentrative meditation is also very useful in many other ways, but I'm pitching it today primarily in terms of making better observations possible.

The second technique which I'll probably get into this morning also is *opening up meditation*, commonly know in English as insight meditation. Once you have started to calm down that storm on the surface, what do you look at? How do you look through the surface to see what you can see?

If these two techniques were the only things I taught you today, you'd have a couple of very interesting tools in life. They would be sufficient to start you working on a science of consciousness. I say *start*, because I have no delusions that anybody is liable to become an expert meditator as a result of a one day workshop, but today's work will give you an idea of the direction you could go and you'll have tools that could start you on the possibility of creating a science of consciousness, either just for yourself, in terms of understanding your own mind and self better and living a better life as a consequence, or in beginning to contribute to a larger social enterprise of disciplined observers actually able to observe their own minds more clearly, starting to share their observations, and contributing to a science of consciousness in a more general sense.

Your work with just these two meditative techniques would ideally be done sitting in a quiet place, usually alone or with other people who are being quiet and meditative. Given how incredibly hurried and stressed out every "normal" person in America is nowadays, teaching anybody a technique where you can sit still and be internally quieter for a few minutes a day is wonderful! It's really good for your health.

External quiet is great, but I've never been interested in living in a monastery, and most people are not, so the question arises, how do you apply this ability more generally? You can learn to quiet your mind and then see things more clearly, so how do you apply it in everyday life? In our afternoon session I'll focus primarily on teaching you how to start applying these skills we work with this morning as part of your everyday life. As part of teaching this, from this point on, insofar as I can remember to do it, I'll be practicing a kind of meditation as I stand here talking to you, rather than just being lost in my usual "thoughtaholic" binge. To the extent to which I am able to do this, my hope, based on my previous experience, is that I'll be able to give you "something" extra, something very difficult to talk about, that will help your learning. That is, I will be modeling mindfulness in everyday life as much as I can.

Basic Concentrative Meditation

Remember, the basic problem is the ongoing, habitual agitation of the ordinary mind. When most people are taught concentrative meditation, it is very common for them, after they try it for a while, to say something like, "I'm not sure I like this stuff. It makes my mind race and go crazy!" Then they have to learn for themselves, or be told that, based on what people who are more experienced understand, "No, meditation does not make your mind race and go crazy. Your mind races and goes crazy all the time; that's your 'normal' state. It was the act of looking at it and/or trying to slow it down that made you aware of something that's happening all the time. Knowing that, you may be able to do something about it."

So basic concentrative meditation is to calm and quiet the

mind. I am tempted to say "still" the mind, but that's far too absolute a way of putting it and erects unnecessary barriers.

The basic instructions are very simple. *Put your mind on one thing and keep it there.* That's it! The actual practice requires a little bit more skill. It requires a little bit more instruction.

To practice quieting and focusing your mind, it's usually quite helpful to quiet and relax your body and your environment to begin with. When you get good at it, you can practice meditation on the New York subway. Meanwhile, any kind of agitated situation makes meditation considerably more difficult because our minds are so driven by our sensory impressions. If there are a lot of things happening outside, you don't have much of a chance. So the general instructions for teaching people concentrative meditation are; first, get in a quiet place. Not where the phone's going to ring, not where the radio or TV is playing, not where people are going to walk in and talk to you, but where you can be undisturbed for the period of practice. That means closing the door, telling your family, if you're doing this at home, "I'm sorry, Mommy or Daddy is not available for the next twenty minutes for anything short of a life threatening emergency. Yes, I still love you, but I need the time alone, okay?" The social practicality part has to be worked out.

The second part of quieting your environment is to reduce the time pressure of a hurried, scheduled life. Very few of us have the luxury of saying, "Okay I'll just sit down and start to meditate for as long as I feel like it." We have an appointment coming up in half an hour or something like that, so time needs to be kept track of. When you get relatively practiced at meditation, it's no big deal to interrupt the meditation for a moment to look at your watch once in a while. When you're initially trying to learn to meditate, that's very distracting to do. Especially because one of the major distractions your mind will throw at you will be constant thought's about "How long have I been doing this? Gee it must be time to stop, surely the fifteen minutes are up!" Giving in to worrying about checking the time is a way of increasing the storm on the surface of the lake and so enhancing the distractions.

The simplest solution to the timing problem is having some kind of timer when you're practicing by yourself. This takes a major load off your mind. Parking meter timers or digital watches with alarm functions or timing functions are readily available.

It's also a good idea, unless a life-threatening emergency comes along, to set a time before you start meditating and stick to it. Otherwise you will often be totally carried away by thoughts on the order of "Well I think the best part of this meditation is over, I might as well get up and write that paper now." Or "Well gee, I've done this enough to deserve a break." That is, your discipline will be undercut by all the rationalizations your mind will create to do something else the instant it gets uncomfortable with meditation. So creating a little discipline that says, "I've set the timer for fifteen minutes, I am not going to get up for fifteen minutes no matter how bad (or how good) it gets!"

So you've isolated yourself socially and physically, you're in a reasonably quiet place, and you've set a timer. So far so good. As another aid, it's generally also easier to practice meditation in a group of like-minded meditators. Not only because somebody else is responsible for keeping track of the time: there are a number of things about sitting surrounded by other people who are meditating that are helpful. Some people might want to theorize at the outer limits about a morphogenetic field a la Sheldrake (Sheldrake 1988), some might want to talk in terms of social and psychological factors, but the immediate sensory reality is that there are those other people sitting there, reminding us that, "Oh! I'm not here to think which of the thirty-seven simultaneous papers I wanted to go hear the most at Tucson III tomorrow, I'm here to meditate — or at least to try to learn to meditate."

So group situations are helpful.

Of course all group situations have a host of psychological and social dynamics that may get very complicated and may help or hinder your learning, depending on the group you get involved with. We'll save that practical problem for later.

Okay, so you've quieted your environment by temporarily eliminating the need to deal with other people, or by being with a group that is doing the same thing you're doing, practicing meditation. You've taken care of the time problem by setting a timer or by allowing someone who is running the group session to take care of the timing for you. I'll perform that function for us today. The next step of quieting is calming and quieting your body.

One of the most basic rules in meditation, until you get very good at it, is to sit still. But your body will say "If I don't scratch this itch, I'll die!" and it will really be convincing. Oh, some small part of your mind may remember that no one has actually ever died from an itch, but the thought that you might can seem terribly convincing at the time!

Or, your body will say, "I'm experiencing a terrible pain! My legs are going to sleep! I think the blood flow is cutting off, I think gangrene is setting in! I'll never get up from here; my legs will drop off." Well, the way a lot of people, especially in the East, meditate, their legs do end up going to sleep, especially if they sit in a cross-legged posture or the full lotus posture. Most traditional Eastern meditation teachers say that nobody has ever died from their legs going to sleep or from the pins and needles pains as the blood rushes back in when you get up. This may be my personal or Western bias, but I don't like that. I take a more pragmatic and "down home" attitude. "You know, the good Lord put all those blood vessels in my leg and His intention was that blood should flow through them! It's healthier that way." So I prefer to tell people to choose meditation postures that are not tests of endurance, that are not going to cause unnecessary (or harmful) pain.

Bodily pain in meditation is a tricky thing. Your body can easily distract you with pain that screams for *immediate* responses to remove the pain, which is completely incompatible with sitting still and focusing your mind. Most of these pains, in real world terms, are absolutely trivial. But they tend to be magnified until they seem just absolutely horrible and you *must* do something about them, *immediately*.

To the degree to which you can learn to sit still and focused through those pains, you can develop great concentrative skill. If the pain is apparently too great, you can actually, as a more advanced meditation practice, make the pain the object of meditation. We'll talk about meditation for pain control sometime later today. But learning to sit through these actually trivial, even though seemingly horrible, pains will teach you a lot about dealing more effectively with unavoidable pains in life — and we all do have some unavoidable pains in life, unfortunately.

If you really think a pain is a sign of genuine physical damage occurring, then the rule is to mindfully adjust your posture, and then go back to meditating immediately. And if you're doing this more than once a minute, you're almost certainly faking it! There is very little likelihood you can really get into a dangerous physical distortion of body position that often. Maybe even more than once a session is too much. You have to judge when it's a real need and when it's a habit of fidgeting that avoids meditating.

So in terms of physical posture today, we're going to use the Western position of sitting in a chair, since we're all sitting in chairs now anyway. If you get really involved in meditation practice and want to stay with the chair modality, you'll probably eventually want to fix up your chair to be more comfortable. Most chairs — this is my personal opinion — are designed for people who have a strong sense of visual aesthetics and no feeling for their bodies at all. I can't believe the number of chairs I've sat in throughout my life, that looked real pretty but were incredibly uncomfortable!

Most chairs, for instance, are designed for a size of person that you are not. Then there are problems with the sitting posture in general. Physiologists tend to tell you that, in evolutionary terms, the upright posture is not been fully engineered yet. Soft cushions you sink into make it worse. A hard cushion is really helpful. If you have a soft cushion, you're not firmly supported and you have to pay more attention to not tilting sideways while sitting on it. A wooden, straight-backed chair is excellent for meditation for most people, perhaps with just a very small amount of padding on it, or something like that.

STUDENT: *I'm sitting here in a little panic because I hear you and other people talk about the importance of sitting absolutely still and quiet, and I think 'Oh my God, I'm going to get into this meditation and then I'm going to have to cough.' Any particular reason for that?*

The Lords of Karma will note that cough in their master log and you'll be punished for it in many lifetimes to come! Now seriously, may a cough during meditation be the worst thing that ever happens to you! If you gotta cough, you gotta cough. Okay? You can make the cough worse, of course . . . here's how you make it worse. As you feel the cough coming on, try to get really panicked about the fact that you're not going to be able to control it, then try and try and try to control it, without succeeding, so when it finally happens you feel really terrible. Firmly believe that everybody in this room will be snapped out of a fantastic meditation experience because *you* coughed. Just as I am about to reach enlightenment, you'll cough! Even worse, it will feel so good to have coughed and relieved that tickling, and that will make you feel really guilty because you not only ruined everyone else's meditation, you felt good about it!

Or you can just cough when you need to and get back to doing the meditation. I recommend the latter way. And perhaps for some of those mild coughs, it might be interesting to make the throat sensations the object of your meditation, in the opening up style we'll talk about later, and see what happens, rather than actually coughing.

I sometimes kid people when I do workshops about things like this. A lot of people, including me, are interested in reaching "enlightenment." Personally I know I'm far from whatever enlightenment is, and I don't really know what enlightenment is, but I am an expert on *endarkenment*. I've had more than fifty years of personal practice and professional study of endarkenment! Knowing how to generate high levels of endarkenment, I figure that the less of that stuff that we do, the less endarkenment we generate, that moves us in the direction of whatever enlightenment is! If you don't make noise, it's naturally quieter. So if you really have to cough, cough. If you have to move, move (mindfully) and get it over with and then go right back to the meditation practice, don't worry about the fact that you moved or coughed or whatever. Everything you add above what is simply necessary to do the action and then come back to the practice is just that much more distraction, that much more endarkenment.

STUDENT: *Isn't the tendency to discipline yourself in any way also a distraction from the profounder purposes of meditation?*

Ultimately it is a distraction, but it's a necessary one for the undisciplined mind, the state we're starting from. From the view of the highest meditation systems, everything I teach you today will really be a higher form of bondage, but it is a necessary step to eventually getting total freedom, total non-dual enlightenment.

STUDENT: *Why do we need to believe you when you say something like that?*

Why do you need to believe me? Because I'm up front on the platform and you're down there in the audience? Because I've been cast in the role of an authority figure? Because as a thoughtaholic I serve my mixed drinks very nicely? It's a good question.

Nobody needs to believe a single thing I say today! Everything I say today is by way of stimulation. Check various parts out for yourself test these ideas I give you. Treat them scientifically as theories to be tested. Are they useful? Fine, use them until they stop being useful. If they are not useful, don't believe a word I've said! I could be quite deluded. But I'm enjoying myself in my delusions, I'll say that!

Delusions undoubtedly exist in the various meditative traditions, as well as in each of our individual lives. One of my bits of practical advice is if you ever get involved with any kind of meditation group that can't laugh at itself, leave! Lack of humor is a very bad sign.

Let's have a five-minute stretch break before we actually start. We tend to get stale as well as intellectually constipated when we sit and listen for too long. As a general tip, a little physical exercise or stretch just before any meditation session can help freshen your mind.

CHAPTER 3

Practice:
Concentrative Meditation

Now I'm going to take you through basic concentrative meditation practice, so find a comfortable posture to sit in. You're going to close your eyes, so if you're more comfortable with your glasses off while your eyes are closed, take them off.

Note to Reader: You will be opening your eyes to read the directions; you can do that quite well. The ellipses (. . .) indicate long pauses between instructions, so you can relax into the instructions . . . rather than just hurrying on from sentence to sentence, as we usually do when reading. Take your time. Get a feeling for following each instruction to at least some degree before going on with the next. This first practice should be spread out over 10-15 minutes, so there's no need to rush.

Begin First Practice of Concentrative Meditation:

Close your eyes . . . Just take a deep breath, and then let it out and just relax as you do so . . . There's no need to be at all tense in basic, concentrative meditation.

Now I've told you an important thing is sitting still, but practically, in the first few minutes when you first sit, after a minute or so you may discover some little adjustment or two you can make that will settle you more thoroughly . . . so that first minute or two can be used for a little more settling.

The basic action in concentrative meditation is to find one object to fix your attention on and to put it there . . . and then, whenever you find your attention has wandered from that object, to gently bring it back to that object. The emphasis being on *gently* . . .

We'll use a classical meditation object for concentrative meditation, namely the natural flow of your breath. Particularly, we'll use the sensation of movement in your chest and belly as the primary thing to direct our attention to . . .

So as I talk and guide you, bring your attention to your belly . . . and just notice that your belly expands and contracts . . . What you're basically to do is to pay open-minded attention to the sensations generated by your belly expanding . . . and contracting . . .

Now there is no need to try to make anything "special" out of this. You don't have to consciously breathe in some particular kind of pattern . . . Just go with the natural flow . . .

If you find your mind tries to interfere with the natural pattern, trying to find some "better" or "proper" pattern of breathing, just be aware of that attempt of interference . . . and then relax . . . and follow the natural expansion and contraction of your belly . . .

There are no shoulds or oughts here . . . The sensation in your belly shouldn't feel like anything in particular . . . or not feel like anything in particular . . . There are no oughts that it ought to be or ought not to be . . . Just experience whatever that sensation is at each moment . . .

If you find that your mind has wandered, so you're thinking about something, or paying attention to something other than the expansion and contraction of your belly, when you realize that, just *gently* bring your attention back to the question of: What do the sensations in your belly feel like, *right now?*

And if your mind has wandered again, again, just gently bring it back . . .

(End First Practice of Concentrative Meditation)

All right, now we'll end this group practice period, so open your eyes, wiggle your body a little, turn on your normal mind, and let me get some questions. I'd particularly like to hear from people who have had difficulty doing this, so I can fine tune the instructions.

STUDENT: *I was wondering, I can feel my body and I try not to concentrate on anything else, and I think I totally blanked out my mind, yet I see features. I don't know who they are, or what they are, but I see features.*

So you have visual images of faces coming up when you do this?

STUDENT: *Yes.*

For learning concentrative meditation, the important thing is to keep paying attention to your object of meditation, the breath in our case now. Perhaps faces will come, faces will go. Pictures may come, pictures may go. Pains may come, pains may go.

STUDENT: *Faces are so interesting! Isn't it significant that I'm seeing particular faces?*

In terms of concentrative meditation, where the goal is to learn to focus properly, anything that arises, other than paying attention to your breath, is a distraction. Don't give voluntary energy to the distraction. On the other hand, don't *fight* distractions. Don't say to yourself, "Ah! It's a distraction, I've got to make those faces go away! I've got to not pay attention to that!" That's actually shifting your concentration to what you're conceptualizing as an obstacle, instead of keeping it on the intended focus of the meditation, the breath in this case. If faces come, let them come. Then gently let them go. If the gods and goddesses come and bow down to you, keep track of your breathing. It's very tricky to try to force things out of consciousness, it's much more straightforward to just keep gently putting the attention back on the object of meditation. Doing that, distractions tend to go on their own.

STUDENT: *Can you indicate how meditation and self-hypnosis relate to each other?*

Comparing this concentrative meditation practice with self-hypnosis is not easy. To begin with, in the real world people used the term "meditation" in a very indiscriminate way to cover a lot of practices, although I'm trying to be more precise today. Then the term "hypnosis" is also used to cover an awful lot of things, and "self-hypnosis" is also used to cover a lot of things. So you can find plenty of overlap in the way various people use these terms at various times.

But here's one major difference. In traditional hypnosis there is an authority figure, someone who knows what's good for you. This authority, the hypnotist, guides the subject into a relaxed, suggestible state to try to produce specific behaviors and experiences, or in therapeutic usage, to fix something in particular. In meditation the authority figure, if you make meditation teachers into authority figures, is only an authority insofar as she can teach you how to do it *yourself*, how to meditate, and does not have lots of specific answers as to what's good for you. This will be an even bigger distinction when we get to opening up, or insight, meditation.

There is a concentration of attention in inducing hypnosis or inducing self-hypnosis, and it's true that the way some people practice self-hypnosis, it sounds more like a meditative procedure than a hypnotic technique (Fromm and Pfeifer 1981). But basically, hypnosis is very goal oriented, with goals of a sort valued in ordinary life, such as losing weight, stopping smoking, being calmer, and the like. Meditation is basically learning to still the ordinary mind, especially in concentrative meditation, to create a ground from where you can observe for yourself, in a deep way, what goes on, how the mind basically functions, rather than knowing the answers as to how the mind works and what's desirable, how to "fix" it, ahead of time. So if any of you are good at self-hypnosis, don't do it now while we are practicing concentrative meditation. It's a wonderful skill you can be proud of, with many important uses, but that's not what we're doing now.[2]

STUDENT: *During the practice I was thinking about prayer, words, and I noticed sensations in my throat and concentrated on them. It got warm, that was interesting. Then my belly got warm so I concentrated there and liked the sensation, it was easier to focus on this warmth in my belly for a while than on my breathing. Was I getting somewhere, or distracting myself?*

Yes, those were all distractions. Remember the mind is so "wonderful" at distracting itself, in everyday life as well as in meditation practice! The mind will readily come up with many more important seeming things you could be doing than following the simple instructions to focus your mind on one, simple thing like the breath. There are no end to the "more important" goals the mind can create moment to moment! Each momentary distraction, each momentary thought, says "This is what you ought to be doing, now!" They're distractions — just keep coming back to the breath sensations in the belly.

STUDENT: *Why is the mind like that?*

Why is the mind like that? All the sages throughout the ages have asked that question!

STUDENT: *That's why I'm asking you!*

Well, I'm going to partly dodge that tough one and draw my answer from the sages who say, "That's simply the way it is." The mind generates one thought after another and it will generate a hundred zillion plus of them in this lifetime. And if you believe in reincarnation, there are umpteen zillion, zillion that went on before that, and, unless you do something like getting enlightened, another umpteen zillion, zillion coming up!

Seriously, the point from the meditation traditions is that you can't effectively deal with the mind by figuring out why it thought what it thought. For instance, if you get distracted by thoughts during meditation, a common thing people do is to try to figure out *why* this particular thought distracted me. Well, you have now started down an infinite path, because before that thought there was another thought, and a previous thought, and there were thoughts about the thoughts and thoughts about the thoughts about the thoughts, *ad infinitum*. When you're distracted by thoughts you certainly can try to figure out why, but by the time you come to an apparently satisfactory answer (or just lose track and finally remember you wanted to meditate) it's minutes or half an hour later before you come back to focusing on the breath — which is what the meditation practice was supposed to be about! All that time has been spent in ordinary thinking, not in practicing meditation. It's much easier to just let thought go.

You can indeed say, as you did, that it's as if the mind has a strong and active motivation to not be still. The constant mental and emotional agitation is what we know as ordinary consciousness. This ordinary mind space — it's called *samsara* in Buddhism or *maya* in Hinduism — is considered a state of illusion in the spiritual traditions. Speaking as a psychologist, I'm not quite so dismissive of ordinary mind, though. Ordinary, busy, "monkey-mind" has its useful and defensive functions. For all the (useless) suffering this agitation has created in our lives, it has useful aspects. We're still alive today after all! Then too the experience of mental quiet is unknown to us, maybe it's dangerous? So there's some natural clinging to habitual mental activity. It's the devil we know rather than the devil we don't know, so there is a lot of motivation to stay with it.

There you get into the whole area of connections between psychotherapy and growth psychologies and meditative practices, which we're only beginning to learn something about. I will avoid going down that path at the moment, but, yes, eventually you can get so good at concentrative meditation that you can produce a state where you have no thoughts for prolonged periods of time. That is a state that is generally described as extremely blissful.

I'll tell you a story about a colleague of mine, Alan Wallace. Alan was a Tibetan Buddhist monk for many years before he came back to the West to finish up his Ph.D. He was once telling me and some other colleagues about how he really liked concentrative meditation. He had been on a six-month, solitary concentrative meditation retreat. On a traditional retreat like this, he stayed in a little, dark, windowless hut and meditated all day and all night long. The retreat support people shoved food through a little set of baffles, so as to not to disturb meditators with any light or sight or sound of another human being, during the six-month retreat. Once every few weeks his meditation teacher would come and talk to him to see how it was going or give pointers, but that was it for ordinary human contact.

Alan was telling us this story as part of a discussion of the disturbances of the ordinary mind, and how difficult they are to control. He reported that one week during his retreat he had so much disturbance in his mind that he broke the very strict rule of never coming out of his hut. He left his hut to go look for his teacher to get more instruction, because he could not keep his mind focused and absolutely free of thought for more than two hours at a time before a thought intruded.

The rest of us who heard this story just rolled on the floor laughing, to Alan's puzzlement. Alan, you poor guy, only two hours without an intruding thought! We had all practiced meditation to various degrees and often found, in our experience, that two *seconds* without a disturbing thought was par for the course, and two *minutes* would be an amazingly quiet meditative mind! But, Alan protested, the older monk in the next hut could do six hours in concentrative meditation before he had a distracting thought! Alan had gotten so good at concentrative meditation that he took mental quiet for granted, and I think it took him a while to realize he was way out of our "ordinary beginning meditators" league.

Now some systems of meditation make a big deal out of achieving prolonged mental quiet, and generally all meditative systems recognize that prolonged mental quiet does produce states of bliss, but in the systems I'm more familiar with, it's considered that quieting the mind is a tool to facilitate insight, not an end in itself. Mental quiet and concentration is a very useful talent. We all have times when our mind is so agitated we're pretty nuts, and it would be wonderful to learn a skill so that even if you can't quiet your mind absolutely, you can at least calm it down a bit. But I see the concentration mainly as a prelude to be able to practice insight or opening up meditation more effectively. And also, again, as an extremely useful skill.

This is one of the interesting things about putting meditation technology in a form more accessible for scientists. Scientists have an ability to concentrate well. You don't make it in your profession if you haven't been able to do a lot of very good concentration of a certain kind to learn the basic material, to focus and discipline yourself, and so forth. On the other hand, the opposite side of that specialized kind of concentration is that it tends to produce a somewhat rigid mindset about what's real and what's not real and about how to do things "properly" and "rationally," a mindset that has to be unlearned in an important way. Continuous thinking becomes a habit that leads to success in one's profession, but can be a major obstacle in learning meditation.

STUDENT: *We had informally talked before class about the*

breathing process itself, how it can involve such things as breathing in through your nose and out through your mouth, or in through one nostril and out the other, etc. It sounds like there is a very interesting technology there. Now are you sure that that's irrelevant? Are we missing something?

It's irrelevant in terms of learning basic concentrative meditation. There are indeed specialized practices. To illustrate the level of complexity that can be involved, you should breathe in to the count of seventeen, hold for the count of three and a half, exhale for the count of nine and hold the breath out for a count of four and a quarter! Don't do that, I'm just making this particular set of values up as an example. There are practices that are further complicated, such as indeed breathing in one nostril and out the other, doing these things in various special body postures, etc. The specialized practices will have a tendency, I'm told, to produce quite specific effects, but the primary thing we're focusing on here, today, is getting the basic concentrative practice down.

Now I should tell you there are two major schools of thought on using the breath as a concentration focus. All of them agree that breath is a very handy as a concentration focus because, unless you're dead, you always have it with you. You keep your meditation practice apparatus in your travel bag all the time, as it were. You can have external objects for your meditation focus — you can look at a candle flame, a religious picture, a thumbtack in the wall, traditional Hindu representations of gods or goddesses, you can focus on circles of colored sand on the ground — there are a zillion things. The basic point for learning the concentration is that once you have selected the target, the object for your meditation session, that's where your attention *stays*. The idea of better targets is generally a distraction. "Gee, I could follow the whole process of breath in and out the nostrils, all the way down to the pit of the stomach, and I could observe the physical expansion and contraction of the entire body . . ." all distractions!

If you said to yourself, "I am going to practice following the breath, its ins and outs, in terms of the expansion and contraction of my belly for this meditation session," then any other aspect of the breath is a distraction. Next time, maybe, you can decide *in advance* that you're going to follow the breath as sensations in the nose. Then stick with it for that session.

Back to our two major schools of thought: one of the major schools follows the expansion and contraction of the belly, and the other major school feels the warming and cooling sensations at the tip of the nostrils as the breath goes in and out. They have gentle, theoretical quarrels as to which system is optimal, which I don't think we need to worry about. I have no idea which is the best way. I prefer focusing on the breath's movement of the belly for an additional psychological reason: we modern Westerners live up in our heads most of the time already! So I figure that anything that helps us pay a little more attention to our actual bodies is probably a good psychological move. I won't get diverted into discussing that now, but there are a lot of data from humanistic and other branches of psychology that indicate living in your whole body is a lot better for you and more satisfying than just living in your head.

So I can't emphasize enough that once the focus object has been selected for a given practice session, that's what you stay with. Even if a god or goddess appears before you and says, "Oh wondrous Mistress or Master, you should be focusing on the pranic (energy) emanations from the left side of the nostril, you are so special!" you can feel excited for a moment, but come back to the breath!

Again I want to emphasize, don't *fight* distractions, you can waste an enormous amount of time. I know, I've wasted an enormous amount of time struggling with distractions, such as ideas of how to improve my meditations, instead of just following the simple instructions!

STUDENT: *When I thought about what I was doing and got off on interesting trains of thought, was I being mindful or was I being distracted?*

One of the meanings of the term "mindful," in everyday life, has to do with thinking, of following the content of what your thoughts are about. That's not the way I'm using it in our work together. I'm using mindful in the sense of being aware, of being attentive to a wide range of phenomena, not just thoughts. Now eventually one could learn to be mindful about thoughts, a kind of meditation I've always personally found very difficult. We'll see this more clearly when we move on to the other major form of meditation practice and the mindfulness in daily life practice. But let's stay focused on concentrative meditation for now.

Don't set yourself some absolute goal that you will not have accomplished anything today unless you can learn to have a state with no thoughts whatsoever. Take it as your normal baseline that you normally have, say, 5,000 thoughts per hour or something like that. If you practice concentrative meditation and you drop the rate by 10%, you're already making a quite significant advance. Perhaps with more practice you learn to focus enough that you drop the rate 20%, so you are only having 80% of the number of thoughts you would normally have.

Eventually you'll also realize that thoughts may come and go, but you can still keep some attention on the belly, on the selected meditative focus. You can see concentrative meditation is not a matter of "I am holding on to this belly sensation and no other awareness will ever get through to me, no matter what!" That leads to a very tense kind of meditation, a mental habit that will be very counterproductive when we work with opening up meditation later. "A thought! God! There, I've killed it!" That's not where we're going. That's essentially being driven by things external to your purpose. Thoughts will come, and if every single one is the occasion for a battle, you've got a long, long struggle ahead.

Okay, here's another way to phrase what we're doing in practicing basic concentrative meditation: We're learning how to set a purpose and actually follow it through. We're starting out with a very simple basic purpose — I am going to focus on my breath and keep in continual contact with that, in a relaxed way. When you master simple purposes like that, then maybe you can have more complex purposes. Then maybe you can learn to do advanced meditative practices, for example: "I'll remember to stay grounded in here-and-now body sensations when my boss is saying things that normally drive me up the wall such that I say stupid things." This is much harder to do than learn to keep with the basic breath.

We're starting out with a basic concentrative process, which provides the foundation for more advanced processes, and also brings great benefits in other areas.

I'll digress here for a moment before we do a bit more practice. Back in 1969, I published my *Altered States of Consciousness* anthology.[3] In the introduction I wrote for the section on meditation, I kind of bragged that I had reproduced there two thirds of the English language scientific literature on meditation. Sounded pretty good — until you realized I had reprinted two of the three articles that I could find in the entire Western scientific literature on meditation. It wasn't much! Meditation research was not exactly a high priority in science at that time.

Then along came an article in this country's most prestigious general scientific journal, *Science*, saying meditation practice had *physiological* correlates (Wallace 1970). Before that, in terms of general Western scientific attitudes, meditation was thought of, on the rare occasions when it was thought of at all, as a schizophrenic-like process, done by little brown men in impoverished countries to escape reality, and hopefully someday progress would cure them of this pathological behavior! (This is not the "politically correct" way to say it, but it succinctly and accurately describes an attitude that had a lot of cultural bias and racism underlying it.) Certainly it was an entirely subjective and crazy thing that was totally unworthy of scientific attention. All of a sudden, it got physiologisized. Overnight, meditation became "real," and it became legitimate to do research on it. Especially if you looked at just the "real" physiological effects of meditation!

Because of this legitimization of meditation research, through putting it in the preferred (or, given many scientists' biases, the "true") explanatory system of physiology, a lot of research on meditation has since been done. Much of this involves no physiological measures, it's plain psychological stuff that could have been done before — but meditation wasn't "real" before. I haven't tried to keep really accurate track, but there are more than 1500 published scientific articles on meditation now. Scientific studies of meditation, not the meditation literature within spiritual traditions, but reasonable-to-good quality scientific studies. The vast majority of these studies find that meditation has all sorts of positive effects in the direction of stress reduction. It doesn't matter too much what you measure: if it's stress related, and people learn to do some kind of meditation, like this basic concentrative kind or Transcendental Meditation (TM), they get better. You can find good overviews of this research in such books as (Murphy and Taylor 1996) and (West 1987).

Now, it's not too clear from the research to date if they get any better than they would if they took twenty minutes a day and, instead of meditating, they did some exercise, or took a nap, or something like that. What is probably a useful general conclusion of the findings so far is that we're ordinarily so stressed out and we're so busy, hurrying, hurrying, hurrying all the time that anything that will make Westerners sit still for twenty minutes a day and relax their mind and body is good for them. It starts cutting into that self-reinforcing stress cycle that has, unfortunately, become a part of "normal" life today. Very few sophisticated studies of meditation have been done to try to get beyond this basic general conclusion. That's the next step in meditation research, to study what various kinds of meditation practice do in a more profound sense than just help us cope with stress — after all, coping with stress is just a small aspect of what meditation is intended to do.

Okay. Are we ready to practice some more? I want to have several brief practice sessions so that I can address the questions that come up in actual practice.

So once again close your eyes — ah, but wait. If you get too sleepy from closing your eyes, which happens sometimes, an alternative is to gently fix your eyes on some point ahead of you. Let's see, I think the standard Hindu tradition here is that you rest your eyes on a spot on the ground one plow length in front of you. If you don't happen to know the standard plow length, it's about six feet. . . . In a situation like this, sitting in chairs in rows, the position is probably the rim of the top of the chair in front of you or something like that.

But if you're going to leave your eyes open, *park* them there. Don't look around — that produces too much stimulation — park them there, rest your gaze there. And don't stare intently. The idea is not to fatigue your eyes — although that could produce lots of far out visual phenomena that make you think you're spiritually advanced. You basically park them in a relaxed position, eyes half-closed. If you don't have a problem with excessive sleepiness, keeping your eyes closed is fine. What I tend to do, and I know what some other meditators tend to do, is that if I'm too mentally agitated when I want to meditate I'll close my eyes, because that does tend to reduce the agitation. If I'm too sleepy, then I'll meditate with my eyes open, parked somewhere, because that tends to raise my level of activation. It's your choice on the eyes this time.

(Reader: This exercise should be spread over 10-15 minutes)

Okay. We begin again. Settle down . . . Shift your attention once again to the sensations of your belly . . . expanding and contracting as you breathe . . . What is that sensation like at this very moment? You don't have to put words on it, but just sense what that's like . . .

Remember, if your mind drifts away, just gently bring it back to the sensation of what's going on in your belly at this moment . . .

Now I could remind you frequently to keep paying attention to the sensations in your belly . . . That would make it somewhat easier . . . and you'd be more likely to think your meditation practice was "successful" . . . But we need to practice keeping our attention focused, with less reliance on external aids, like my reminding you . . . So I'm going to give us five or ten minutes of quiet . . .

(5-10 minutes of quiet)

Let your experience center around just remembering to come back and focus on the sensations of breathing in your belly . . . Just sensing how they are, moment to moment, as continually as possible . . . But relaxed . . .

If you've gotten distracted from the sensations of breathing, just gently bring your mind back . . . If you've started thinking about something — the thought perhaps saying "This is a brilliant, wonderful, once in a lifetime thought that absolutely must be pursued!" — just gently relax and come back to your breathing . . . You'll never lack for thoughts later in life . . .

There are occasional noises from outside the room . . . or from other people coughing or moving . . . but you don't have to have absolute quiet to keep focusing your attention on your breathing . . .

Now I'm going to move around a little up here . . . Since you're not deaf, you hear me, but don't pay any particular attention to that — you don't have to block it — but just keep coming back to the sensation of your breath . . .

Okay . . . Bring yourself back to your ordinary state of

focus now . . . Open your eyes if they're closed, and let's see how that went.

STUDENT: *This worked even better for me than it did in our previous practice. My mind was much calmer and I liked the state produced. I don't know whether to call it joy or bliss or just calm or what. Don't the meditation traditions talk about joy being higher than bliss or something like that?*

I have wondered all my life about the distinctions between "joy" and "bliss" in the traditions, and have never clearly figured out what was meant. There is a certain inherent satisfaction in being calm. How many people have noticed a certain satisfaction in being calm?

(Many hands are raised.)

It's funny in a way. Usually when we say joy, we think of some specific kind of exciting happiness. But there is a very real sense in which you might say that when you calm your mind, nothing's happening, and gee, it's nice! Especially compared to the constant hectic quality of ordinary consciousness! If you get really deep into and accomplished with Hindu yoga or Buddhist meditation practices, they will distinguish things like bliss from joy. They'll distinguish high meditative states (they're called jhana states) like one in which you experience bliss, joy and equanimity as being a lower state than one in which you experience bliss and joy but not equanimity. Good luck on following this now, I don't!

STUDENT: *I went the other way, I found it harder to keep my mind at all focused this time and had greater difficulty keeping distractions from coming in, whereas the first time I did feel a good sense of calm and focus. I feel a sense of guilt at how I've gotten worse!*

A sense of guilt?

STUDENT: *A sense of guilt in not achieving a moment of quietude.*

Tell me more. Why do you feel guilty at not quieting your mind for a moment?

STUDENT: *I guess, in my arrogance, I look at my mind as being just this little asset that should solve all the world's problems, and I should be in charge of that asset. Instead I kept getting carried away on thought trains all the time that weren't relevant to what we're doing. I couldn't let go of them.*

We do get hooked on our thoughts! Remember the example I mentioned while I was guiding you through this practice? When thoughts interrupt my attempts to sit calmly, they usually present themselves with the quality, "I'm not just an *ordinary* thought. I'm a really *brilliant* insight, and if you don't really pay attention to me you'll probably lose this once in a lifetime opportunity to finally understand everything important!"

The attitude I try to take for dealing with such distractions is to remember that, basically, thoughts are real liars in this respect! *Every* trivial thought presents itself as important! Once in a great while, I really have a very important thought during meditation. One of my meditation teachers, Sogyal Rinpoche, has departed from strict tradition on this, for he advises that if you have this problem, keep a notebook beside you, and if its a really brilliant thought, write it down. Then *forget it* and go back to the practice of the meditation. I think this is brilliant advice and it's helped me.

STUDENT: *I had an interesting experience: I was wandering in my mind when all of a sudden I got this stabbing sensation in my body. Then I couldn't pay attention to anything but that sensation for a while. But it's funny, because I was even more concentrated on that pain than I had ever been on the breath.*

It's being more physical that brought you back from the thought distractions, yes. There are other forms of meditation — concentrative meditation style — that involve intense physical activity because that will concentrate you by forcibly grabbing your attention. So, for instance, if you want to concentrate on your body sensations, if you hired some big, burly guy with a club to chase you around and try to hit you, you would be marvelously focused as you ran and felt those body sensations! Strong physical sensations are much more "concrete" and so are easier to focus on than the gentle sensation of breathing or the "higher" mental processes, even though the latter cause us more trouble when out of control. So the stabbing sensation was a help to you in a way.

Physical sensations are a great help for learning meditation. In the Buddhist tradition, for instance, they talk about six different realms of existence, some of which are unembodied realms, like a god realm and a demigod realm. Forget about the ultimate reality or lack of it of these realms for now, just take them as psychological states. As Westerners, labels like "god realm" and "demigod realm" sound appealing, maybe that's what we mere mortals want to achieve, but . . . The tradition is that those unembodied realms aren't as good for achieving enlightenment as the human realm, because having a body gives you a certain stability that helps you focus — helps bring you back from potentially infinite mind wandering. At a simple level, its harder for me to go to sleep if I'm meditating sitting up, because, when my head starts to fall, as that stage one EEG kicks in and the paralysis system knocks out my muscle tone, that wakes me right back up. I'm told that some yogis who really don't want to go to sleep at all while meditating put a glass of cold water on their head. As long as you're fairly awake, it takes almost no attention to keep your head upright and so the glass stays on, but when your head nods, that splash of cold water in the lap is very stimulating! And the ones who really, really, do not want to go to sleep, I'm told, meditate in the cross-legged lotus posture on the edge of a precipice, so they have a lot of motivation to stay awake . . . I'm not into extremes like that!

STUDENT: *I find it quite pleasurable to meditate this way, there is sort of a rhythm of being more or less integrated into my body, much more integration of mind and body than I normally experience.*

Good! It is pleasurable to tune into your body. Now I'm assuming that everyone in this room has at least a bachelor's degree from college, and probably one or two advanced degrees also. How much of that did you earn by becoming more aware of your body?

Our educational system rewards talk power. The faster you can talk and the more cleverly you can talk, the more likely you are to get an advanced degree. Now, that's all right in some ways: there is a lot of useful knowledge that can be conveyed through words. But the fact remains that we are embodied creatures. We tend to forget that at times, especially when we're thinking (essentially all the time), but there is something below the head. Getting in touch with that something, your body, does put you in touch with a kind of inherent pleasure in existence. In fact you can accurately say that, in too many ways, we live in a world of words, of abstractions, and that cuts down the joy of life.

In the East they have the concept that we are living in illusion. *Samsara*, again, is the Buddhist term and *maya* is the roughly equivalent Hindu yoga term for it. These terms are usually translated for Westerners as ontological in nature, meaning that the world is an illusion, it's not real. But that's not quite the point. There are many philosophical schools within Buddhism and Hinduism, of course, just as in any major system of thought, and some of them think that the material world is illusory and unreal in some sense, but that's not really the main point of maya or samsara. The real, psychological point is that we habitually, "normally," live so much in abstractions, in concepts, in theories, in beliefs, that we pay very little attention to the actual, real world around us. We mistake our theories about the world, as it were, for the actual data about the world — that's living in illusion, for many of these abstractions we live in are badly distorted representations of reality. And that has two consequences. One is that it generates *karma*. It leads us to do stupid things because of poor contact with and perception of what's actually going on in our lives, which produces consequences that affect us sooner or later. Karma basically means cause and effect. Everything has a cause and an effect, even if not immediate or obvious. The second consequence, immediately relevant to the point you just raised, is that it cuts us off from an essential joy in life.

There is a joy in the actual taste of vanilla ice cream that does not come from knowing the chemical formula of vanilla. There is a joy, an inherent aliveness in the body that you can experience if you pay attention to your body. But if you live up in your head, in your words all the time, you don't notice it.

Since I retired from the University of California at Davis several years ago now, except for one year in the Chair of Consciousness Studies at the University of Nevada in Las Vegas, I've been teaching half time at the Institute of Transpersonal Psychology in Palo Alto. This is an institution that I monitored and supported from its very beginning, some twenty-five years ago, because it was quite an amazing idea in education. ITP offers an accredited Ph.D. in Transpersonal Psychology,[*] but instead of just teaching students more and more clever words, like practically all graduate schools do, there is equal emphasis, from the very beginning of the program, on educating your body and educating your emotions! That's really unique. That has been expanded to educate the spiritual, social and creative sides of students too. The idea that your emotions could be intelligent, that your body could be intelligent: that's really important.

Let me give you a personal example of why this broad education is so important. Years ago I saw a demonstration of the Japanese martial art of Aikido, and I was really intrigued. The self-defense aspect of it appealed to me. The philosophy behind it struck me as very noble. The fact that it was a meditation in action struck me as very interesting and clearly of practical value, so I arranged for a black belt instructor in Aikido, Alan Grow, to come up to UC Davis a couple of days a week and teach a class. Well, Alan was fantastic. He was so graceful, so effective and so powerful in what he did. And within two weeks — I could "explain" Aikido much better than him.

I could relate it to developments in psychology, to different world religions, to various philosophies and so forth. I've had a "black belt" in talking since about the time I was ten years old. But what I kept noticing was that while I could outtalk him, I couldn't do anything, while he could throw me across the room with what seemed like a mere wave of his little finger! I kept noticing this disparity between my talking knowledge and my real knowledge when I was thrown across the room: that was a strong enough experience to make me notice something!

It took me several years of study and practice to realize that collecting lots of *words* about Aikido was not particularly relevant, and, indeed, was usually extremely misleading. Slowly I began to learn how to "pay attention at a bodily level" (the intellect can't phrase this kind of knowledge satisfactorily) as to what was going on. Eventually I actually learned to do some Aikido instead of just being good at talking about it. This was first major introduction to the reality of kinds of knowledge that were not intellectual, and how important educating these other parts of ourselves is.

Remember this conference we're at, Tucson III, is really a thoughtaholic orgy! We're going to have some stuff thrown at us that is really intoxicating, heady, exciting stuff! My head's going to explode before the end of the week; I know that — unless I'm real careful . . . I'll probably be skipping some sessions. A wise thoughtaholic tries to "drink" in moderation — but still my head's going to explode, I'm going to have some fine intellectual drunks! Judging by my past experiences of conferences, I also know that after I get home, I'm going to notice that somewhere I forgot my body. I remember having one when I got on the plane to come here, but it got lost somewhere, and it'll take me a while to regain it.

One of the things that concentrative meditation will do, especially when we're using a body function like breathing as our meditative focus, is that it starts to bring us into our bodies. The body does have a inherent joy. It also has certain wisdom, which, if you never pay any attention to your body, you never get much of. So beginning to focus in on the breath starts to put you in touch with that joy and wisdom — as well as clearer and more accurate perception of the unpleasant aspects of body sensation too.

STUDENT: *I didn't expect this, but I feel more connected with the other people in this room as we meditate together, even though we don't really know each other.*

If you feel a little less alienated as we do this, that's wonderful! Of course most of us are strangers in the ordinary meaning of the term, but the meditative traditions tell us that one of the things we will discover for ourselves, if we get good at meditation, is that we are really intimately connected, nowhere near as separate as we think. I've even been told by some of my teachers, for example, that everybody in this room has Buddha nature. Our perception of Buddha nature is very poor, this shining nature is clouded over by our thoughts and feelings and preoccupations, but it's there in reality. That's rather theoretical stuff for me, I'm afraid, I've had no direct experience of that, but it's an inspiring idea. I much prefer a system that says our basic nature is Buddha nature to one that says our basic nature is original sin! Grounding in the body, coming back to the simple reality of your breathing, takes energy away from habitual mental processes that actively create the "stranger" quality, the extra and unnecessary alienation, so perhaps we are lessening an illusion.

STUDENT: *Can we meditate on things other than the breath?*

Yes, you can do concentrative meditation on other things, other foci. For instance, if you had some external object to focus on, you might learn the concentration skills just as well, but that doesn't quite bring you into your body as much.

People can even meditate on ideas as a focus, like "Truth" or "Justice" or "Mercy." That kind of practice is something I've avoided like the plague, though, because I'm too abstract already! That's the last thing I need. I need to continue to get in my body and my senses, and pay attention to reality, and I think an awful lot of us here today are like me in that need.

We have to be careful not to get too intellectual here, it's a constant temptation among thoughtaholics like us.

I do want to introduce one other kind of meditation before lunch time. Let me ask you before I start that though, are there any particular questions on anything you don't understand about the technique I've introduced so far, especially in terms of how to do it?

STUDENT: *I'm getting sleepy when we practice. What can I do?*

Yes, sleepiness during meditation practice is a very common problem. You can do various things. I've already said, for instance, you can meditate with your eyes open, which can help. Or if you've started with your eyes shut you can open them and park them somewhere if you feel very sleepy, close them again when you don't feel so sleepy. But if you're sleepy enough, you'll still get sleepy, eyes open or not.

I used to sometimes bite my tongue when I got too sleepy, just to get a little jolt of sensation going through there, not enough to cause injury, but even that doesn't always help.

You can regard sleepiness as a terrible enemy and work *really* hard to concentrate and keep coming back to the focus of concentration. That may develop great skill in you, but I'm a little reluctant to recommend that because it tends to make meditation too harsh. That's why when I'm guiding you in practice I keep saying to you, *gently* bring your attention back when you notice it's wandered. People can get into a very effortful style of concentrative meditation, "I'm going to focus on this no matter what!" and this creates enormous tensions and can produce all sorts of other side effects that are not good. Also, one of my meditation teachers, Sogyal Rinpoche, says that sleepiness in meditation is usually a distraction but sometimes it means it might be a good idea to lie down and take a nap for a few minutes and then meditate! We bring a little reasonableness in here.

Be reasonable too about the fact that if perhaps your experience wasn't as good the second practice time, it's no big deal. Especially when you're just beginning. There are going to be enormous variations from one meditation to the next. Eventually as your mind gets clearer in observing itself, it will produce very rewarding experiences, but still there will be enormous variation within a session. I'll have sessions, for example, where my mind will get crystal clear within a few seconds, and I think, "Hey, I'm getting pretty good here! This is going to be a really good session!" Half an hour later I realize that immediately following that thought I began thinking about designing an extension on my treehouse or about an article I wanted to write and totally forgot about meditation.

STUDENT: *I'm having this problem meditating on the sense of breathing for a very simple reason. Breathing is important for me as I'm asthmatic, so I'm very concerned about exactly how my breathing is going. If a change in the quality of sensation occurs I automatically analyze it to see if it means an attack might be coming on, whether I should take medication now, and so forth. What should I do?*

You do have a special problem there. You're too "educated" about breathing. I mean educated in the body sense, not just in an intellectual sense. For you, concentrative meditation might perhaps be better done on some external object. Some simple little thing — a thumb tack on a wall — or something like that. If you use an external object, look at it *gently*, don't stare in a visually, ocularly concentrated way because ocular tension will cause a lot of eye fatigue. The eye fatigue will make all sorts of "interesting" things happen and you may think you're having great spiritual experiences but it's just eye fatigue. Some meditation systems, I think, "cheat" and use these visual effects as a way of encouraging people, sort of a

"Oh! It changed shape and size? You're getting there, it's spiritual perception" kind of thing. Well, that happens when you stare fixedly at anything, whether it's a spiritual symbol like a crucifix or a simple thumb tack. Maybe it's good psychology to use the effects to encourage people, maybe not. But an external object might work better for you.

STUDENT: *Does concentrative meditation work if you focus on a sound, a sacred word or something like that?*

Using a word, using a sound as focus is called mantra meditation in yoga and Buddhism. In some ways it's a little easier than using something like your breath because you have to put a little more active effort into it. Especially if you're doing it out loud, rather than just producing an auditory image — "audiolizing," a parallel to "visualizing," is the word I've always wanted to introduce — in your mind. Traditionally, the sounds/words used as foci are special, mantras are sacred sounds (Blofeld 1977). They're sounds that are supposed to have some cosmic significance, to actually reflect or resonate with spiritual processes. I have no idea whether that's true or not. But if you're raised in one of the cultures where you think that's the case, a mantra will probably have some special significance to you; otherwise it's just a focus point. Mantra meditation is especially neat, powerful and pleasurable, in group settings.

Transcendental Meditation (TM) is a form of mantra meditation. TM is the meditation the Maharishi Mahesh Yogi, known to many of you as the Beatles' guru, introduced to the West. In initiating and instructing you, they give you a particular mantra, apparently chosen on the basis of your sex and age, and you repeat it over and over, not out loud but in your mind, in your practice sessions. I practiced it for about one and a half years and found it useful (Tart 1972). TM is an interesting blend between pure concentrative meditation and opening up/insight meditation, but we don't have time to get theoretical, interesting as it would be. It's time to move on.

CHAPTER 4

Opening Up Meditation, Vipassana

Insight *meditation* is a common term used for the second major kind of meditation. "Insight" is a little misleading for us Westerners, as we tend to put a very psychological quality on "insight." Insight is thought of as: "Oh! That's why I treated my sister that way as a child — my unresolved conflict!" — something like that. Insight is being used here in the much more general sense of a clearer than usual perception of what is actually happening at the moment. Another common term for this kind of practice is *opening up meditation*, and it doesn't have the overly psychological connotations of insight.

If you think about what I said earlier about the way we tend to live in our abstractions, in our concepts and emotions, in our mental and emotional reactions to our mental and emotional reactions *ad infinitum*, then, since attention is limited, we're not paying very clear attention to moment-by-moment reality, we're not open to whatever is. We're highly specialized, highly filtered people, just taking in what we think is important. I could go on at length with my world simulation model of consciousness which would illustrate this in detail, in modern psychological terms (Tart 1987) (Tart 1991) (Tart 1993), but I'll resist this thoughtaholic temptation for all of us because we want to get on to the actual practice of opening up/insight meditation.

Opening up meditation or insight meditation is learning to pay attention to what *is*, without trying to force the moment's experience to be anything we think it *should* be or keep it from being what we think it *shouldn't* be. The classical Buddhist form of this is called vipassana. Since "insight" tends to have the wrong connotations and "opening up" is a little awkward, I'll generally use the term vipassana in referring to this kind of meditation from now on, unless I want to emphasize some other aspects of the practice.

In its purest form, the instructions for vipassana meditation are very simple. Again you sit quietly, don't move and then you simply pay open-minded attention to whatever is, moment-by-moment, with equanimity, with no attachment or aversion to whatever comes up and no attempt to manipulate whatever comes up.

Now as pure instructions, that's very neat, but it's hard to learn that way. Suppose your mind wanders on to preparing a shopping list for your next trip downtown. Well, that is what is at the moment, isn't it? But we are already very good at letting our minds be taken over by trains of thought, so there must be more to it than that! Dealing with thought can be tricky in vipassana meditation, just as in concentrative meditation.

So the way vipassana is usually taught is as a compromise between concentrative meditation and pure vipassana meditation. Rather than tell you to simply sit still and pay open-minded attention to anything that happens to come along, with no attempts at control, they give you some restrictions. The usual restriction is to pay attention to whatever body sensations happen to come along. Body sensations *per se* cover a very wide range, so you're getting practice at broadening your attention, the vipassana part, but they are distinct enough from, say, preparing your shopping lists, that you know essentially when you stopped doing vipassana and wandered off into ordinary mental functioning.

This typical form of vipassana is what we'll practice. You'll sit still again and try not to move unnecessarily. You can have your eyes closed or you can park them in a relaxed, half open position somewhere. Then you'll begin to pay attention to whatever sensation in your body happens to be prominent at the moment. If there are several prominent ones, then pay attention to the most prominent one.

Now don't get hung up, if you have, say, three sensations, on thinking about which of these things is actually the most prominent sensation that you should focus on. That way lies madness! Just focus on whatever body sensation happens to be strong at the moment.

In vipassana, there are no "good" sensations and no "bad" sensations. There are not particular sensations you're supposed to experience, or particular sensations you're not supposed to experience. One of my traps, for instance, when I do this kind of vipassana meditation, is that I tend forget this instruction and fall prey to the automatized forces of attraction and aversion. I might sometimes be aware of sensations of soreness in my butt (from sitting for a long time), for example, and then think (or find myself thinking, it's not usually a conscious choice), "That's not a very spiritual sensation. Surely there should be a more spiritual sensation coming along in my body that I should be focusing on?" Nope, that's just distraction, just craving for "special experience" and aversion to unpleasant experience. Such automatic yielding to craving and aversion is, from the Buddhist point of view, a major source of our unhappiness.

Pay attention to whatever the strong sensation of the

moment is. When that sensation of the moment arises on its own, it comes, it arises. That is, you don't try to make any particular sensation. If it gets stronger, let it get stronger. If it gets weaker, let it get weaker. If it changes, let it change. When that sensation goes, let it go. Don't try to hang on to it. Don't say things to yourself like "Hmm, this vibration in my heart, I really like that, I must be making meditative progress . . . now it's fading. No! Now let me concentrate more and make it last." No, things come, they come — things go, they go. Neither hold on to anything nor reject anything.

If a "pain" comes along, instead of saying to yourself, "Oh my God! It's a *pain*, I'm going to die, and I've got to fight it!" just pay attention to what it actually is. It might actually turn out to be something quite interesting. It might actually turn out to be an interesting "pain" with interesting qualities that you never knew that pains had, or it might actually be something quite new.

So if you pay attention to whatever comes along, when it goes and something else replaces it, that's fine. If the sensation is a clear sensation, a sudden itch in your foot that kept you from having your mind wander, for example, that's fine. Pay attention to *exactly* what that feels like.

Now when I say "pay attention," or "pay clear attention," an analogy I like to sometimes use to illustrate what I mean is this: Suppose you have a friend who is a real gourmet cook, who makes really delicate and delicious stuff, very subtly flavored, delicious things. If you went over to your friend's house and he said to you, "I've prepared this new dish with a very delicate taste. I'd like you to try it and give me your opinion," what would you do?

Well, you'd certainly try to stop thinking about what happened at the office that day, or what's going on in your lab. You'd try to bring your attention to your body, to your mouth, to your senses of taste and smell, and you'd just try to open your senses to what the experience would actually be when you tasted the new food. That's the way you would open your-self to something delicate. If you were thinking about some-thing else at the time, you know you wouldn't really be able to appreciate anything delicate or subtle, only a grossly pow-erful flavor would really get your attention. If you have pre-conceptions — "Oh I bet this will be tart, or I bet this will be sour," or something like that — that's going to get in the way. If you have preferences — "Oh I hate new foods. No, I don't want to try it! I know I won't like it" — that's not going to let you appreciate what it really is.

So when I say pay clear attention to whatever sensations come along in an open-minded way, take that attitude you would take as this friend offers you this really delicious and subtle concoction, and you want to know what it really tastes like. What it really feels like as you crunch on it, what it really smells like, how your body reacts to it, and so forth.

Now I don't have any gourmet treats to pass out, unfortu-nately, but we're going to use the sensations from your own body as our focus in vipassana. So let's do this and see how it goes.

CHAPTER 5

Practice: Vipassana

(The following practice should be spread over 5-15 minutes)

So again, settle down, and either close your eyes or park them . . . Take a moment to wiggle and adjust so you get comfortable if you need to . . . And now turn your attention to your body . . . First, for a second, just sense your whole body . . . Then notice some particularly strong sensation, and tune in to it. What does it actually feel like *at this moment*? . . . If it lasts, and you keep paying attention to qualities of it, that's fine . . . If it's starting to fade or change and something else is coming in, that's fine . . . Pay attention to what comes in . . .

Breathing, of course, is a body sensation, and that might be the prominent sensation sometime . . . But there is no need to hold on to breathing to the exclusion of anything else . . . When it's prominent, fine . . . When something else comes in, fine . . .

Again, as much as possible, sit still and just savor . . . just taste, whatever the prominent body sensation is . . . Sensations might come and go rapidly . . . and they might come and go slowly . . . Whatever happens naturally is fine . . . You just tune in to it.

If you find you've wandered off into thinking about something, instead of actually paying attention to sensations, come back to body sensations . . . Come back gently . . . If a sensation of sleepiness comes, fine, pay clear attention to it. . . . What are the body aspects of sleepiness? Can you focus on the quality of that body sensation?

Okay, bring your attention back to its normal deployment now. Let me see if there are any questions about how to do this, or reports of difficulties, or good things in doing it, and so forth, so we can fine tune this practice a bit more.

STUDENT: *I find myself wanting to put labels on these things. My mind just compulsively analyzes and labels my sensation with words. Is there a way to get beyond that?*

So you find yourself wanting to put labels on everything. I'm sure you're quite unique in doing that! (*Everyone laughs!*) I hereby pronounce you normal!

Yes, there is a way to get beyond that. First off — don't fight putting labels on it. If you try to fight that process, you just increase its strength and create a lot of extra tension and distraction. Accept the fact that part of your mind is putting labels on sensations and keep coming back to what's the quality of the sensation, moment-by-moment.

So, you're starting to eat this delicacy that your friend has prepared and your mind starts to say, for example, "Oh, a little taste of basil." Now if that verbal analysis stays small, uses just a little part of your attention, you can still pretty much taste what it actually is. But for most, if not all of us, there is too much of that tendency, of course, this idea, this verbal label, of "a little taste of basil" will then sweep you off into an all-absorbing intellectual and pseudo-sensory simulation process where you don't notice the continued subtle variation of the flavors, where you're now immersed in ideas about the taste of basil. So as I said, don't try to fight this verbal analysis; that won't help. But do try to just pay less attention to it, not by trying to force your attention away from the distraction, the verbal activity, but by focusing more on the actual flavor, the here-and-now qualities of the actual moment-by-moment sensations.

There is a technique of deliberate *noting*, often used with vipassana meditation. You recognize that your mind's going to analyze and label experiences on its own — and likely get lost in the labels — so you use a different, deliberate and conscious kind of labeling, usually referred to as noting. Such deliberate, conscious noting makes this verbal activity much less toxic and distracting.

One form of the basic noting procedure is that is whenever you notice that you're distracted in thought, instead of staying caught up in the particular thought, carried away by it, just mentally say something to yourself like "Labeling," or "Automatic labeling," or "Thinking," i.e. *consciously* note what you're doing. This conscious noting reminds you to stop giving attention to thinking/analyzing. It's not so much that you actively suppress the thought; you label what you've been doing and then let the thought (and the conscious label) go. Then go back to paying clear attention to the dominant sensation of the moment. So your experiential flow might be something like: sensation → next sensation → next sensation → thinking starts → thinking goes on for a while → consciously noting that you are labeling or analyzing → next sensation → next sensation → thinking starts → consciously noting that you're analyzing or labeling → next sensation, and so forth. Conscious noting tends to take some or all of the intensity automatized thought distractions away. Some of the references in Appendix 1 to source books on meditation practice will go into the noting technique in detail.

I can't remind us enough that *we're so attached to our thoughts!* We've become so convinced they're so very important! I used to think, for instance, that if I had a good idea I'd better jot it down fast and think about all its implications because maybe there is a limit on the number of good ideas, and I might not have any more! What nonsense! I've come to believe that ideas are actually cheap, there is no end of them. And yet it's so easy to get caught up in fighting the thinking process, especially as you get better at experiencing moments of meditative calm and aliveness and realize how much the richness of life is taken away by continual ideas, ideas that keep us living in an abstraction instead of the actual sensory reality, ideas that mean we're constantly reading and thinking about the recipe for that delicious meal set before us instead of tasting it!

But fighting to get rid of thoughts, trying to actively suppress them, is the wrong thing. It's more that you have to shift your attention to what's important. I have a lot of thoughts come and go while I'm meditating, but occasionally I reach a point where even when a thought is happening, I can usually keep at least some of my attention on the meditation focus. I don't get completely lost in the thought for seconds or minutes or hours the way I used to. When I first started learning to meditate, a thought would come which would trigger a thought, which would trigger a thought, which would trigger a thought — *ad infinitum* — and I'd be lucky if within fifteen minutes I got back to actually paying any attention to the actual meditation focus! Now most of my chain-of-thought distractions seldom go on for more than a few seconds before I recognize them and come back to the meditation focus. So, improvement is possible, even for thoughtaholics like you and me.

If you feel this process is difficult when you're doing it for the first time today, please don't get discouraged. It's normal for it to feel difficult. Remember the example I gave you, "I hate this meditation thing because it makes my mind race!" No, your mind's been racing your whole life! You can live with that, but you can learn something for slowing down and getting closer to actual sensory reality — which, as we will see, is very nice.

STUDENT: *Yes! I have a problem with conflict that I'm having here. The conflict is that we're doing, as I understand it, an exercise to be aware of what's going on and to focus on what is actually going on. And that means that I need to look at it and label it — and yet not label it. What I found was happening was that for example I would find that I would have a sensation, for example, in my left knee. I focus on that instead of thinking about my previous thought, but then I find I'm automatically thinking about it, calling it an "itch" or "warmth" or something. Eventually I recognize that I got caught in this labeling, but coming back to my knee, the sensation that started all this is often gone! I'm confused about labeling and what to do.*

Sensations often disappear very quickly, and you will indeed miss "tasting," "savoring" the fading process if you're lost in the label your mind has involuntarily put on it. Slow or rapid changing or fading of a sensation is part of the natural process, it's okay.

We have such a strong tendency to get lost in thoughts! Face it, we're all end products of many consecutive cullings and selections of the academic system, cullings and selections which reward people addicted to thought. That leads us to think that thoughts are reality. So when I ask you to focus on sensations, as you noticed, your mind tends to then immediately put an intellectual label on the sensation and then get lost in thoughts about the thoughts about the thoughts, etc.. That kind of analysis is what got you the grades that got you where you are today!

Now let's look at this from the perspective of my working theory of the way the mind functions — I don't know that this is an ultimate truth, but it's a model that makes intellectual sense of a lot of things about the mind. My model (Tart 1987) (Tart 1991) (Tart 1972) (Tart 1975) (Tart 1991), like that of many others, is that we have a relatively fixed and limited amount of attention available, so if you take some of that attention and put it here, there is less of it to put (or be automatically drawn) over there. When a sensation happens and the intellectual labeling/analysis/chain-of-thought process automatically occurs, it literally uses up a lot of your attention, and so awareness of the actual sensation gets less. In many instances practically all attention may be gobbled up by the intellectual processes and you lose moment-to-moment reality and richness of the sensation. It's quite possible to live a life in your head, where your body is a very minor appendage, very seldom contacted except in extreme circumstances. What we're doing today is specific training to learn a greater degree of flexibility, to have more control over where your attention goes so it isn't automatically and always diverted into intellectual abstractions. Okay?

STUDENT: *Are you teaching us to use right brain functions rather than left ones? Is that what meditation is like?*

No. I wouldn't liken it to the left and right brain. Because the left and right brain distinction was so mythologized in popular culture so quickly, I got rather disillusioned with it. I don't want to theorize about brain correlates of meditation too much, but again, we're in the habit of intellectualizing. To be able to intellectualize, to intellectually analyze, is one of the greatest talents human beings can have. To be able to do nothing but have things automatically intellectualized all the time, with no choice about it, is to lose much of the richness of life and to lose access to all sorts of other abilities. To return to our earlier analogy, we want to be able to find those hidden treasures under the surface of the water. Vipassana meditation, this opening up or insight meditation, is specific training to keep coming back to the ongoing flow of sensations of the moment, instead of living a life where you have one sensation, then dozens or hundreds of thoughts and emotions, a second sensation, five hundred thoughts and emotions, etc. Vipassana is learning to keep coming back to the immediate reality of the here-and-now. And it's not easy. We're not used to coming back from the intellectual stuff, but this is specific training for doing it, and you can get better at it.

Again, I had extreme difficulties in learning this when it was first taught to me, even when it was repeatedly taught to me. My thoughts were so important! I couldn't possibly let them go. But I'll tell you a funny thing. I have gotten much better at bringing my attention back to the present moment. In a sense, I have practiced being "non-intellectual" for many years now, but it hasn't made me dumb! Amazingly enough I seem to hold my own intellectually: in fact, I think the quality of my intellect is now considerably better than it used to be, because it has a lot more grounding in factual reality than it used to have. So I'm encouraging you, but it's not easy.

STUDENT: *I had an experience similar to the other questioner. I noticed a rather sharp pain under my rib cage and I focused on it. It then turned out to be interesting, instead of "pain." After ten seconds or so I noticed that the pain had actually disappeared.*

That's a very interesting experience. So the pain came, you focused on it, it changed, and then it went away. At the risk of strengthening your addiction, fellow thoughtaholics, I want to give you an important principle here. This is something I learned from my friend Shinzen Young, who as I said earlier, is one of the best meditation teachers around, not only because of the depth of his own experience that he draws from, but because he has adapted traditional Buddhist and other Eastern ideas to Western terms for better communication. He thought very seriously about how Buddhism had adapted when it went into sophisticated cultures like China and Japan to see if he could find ideas for facilitating its movement into the West. As a result he tends to put many Buddhist concepts into psychological or mathematical language — it makes them a lot more accessible.

One thing Shinzen has formulated is the relation between pain, suffering, and resistance. Consider the following approximate equation he's developed:

S = P x R

S is suffering, P is pain (pain in terms of actual neurolog-
ical sensations) and R is psychological resistance. Suffering is
a psychological/experiential concept. Suffering — we all know
what suffering is! — we've had so much of it, right? Pain is a
physiological variable, how frequently those nerves are actually firing, the chemicals being released to irritate nerve endings,
and so forth. Pain is the actual physical sensation. Resistance
we also know about. We're all quite good at resisting things!
Resistance is a psychological variable again.

Now just imagine for the moment that we could easily
quantify each of these three variables. From his and others'
meditative experience, Shinzen is formulating the relationship
in the above equation. To illustrate its consequences, if you
have a pain of, let's say, one unit, and pain really freaks you
out, so as soon as you feel that pain it's "Oh, my God, I'm in
pain!" so you have ten units of resistance, you experience ten
units of suffering, even though there's only one unit of pain!
It can get worse. If you actually have a strong pain, say you're
passing a kidney stone or the like (I have more personal
understanding of this than I wish I had!), say you've got ten
units of pain and you're totally freaked out about it, you're
really resisting (ten units of resistance) you have a hundred
units of suffering!

On the other hand, let say, you've got a fairly severe pain,
you've got ten units of pain, you broke a leg or something like
that, but somehow, through meditative training or whatever,
you accept the fact that yes, it hurts badly, but you actually
know how to kind of meditate on the quality of the sensation.
Instead of freaking out about it, you only have a resistance of
one. Then, even though you have ten units of pain, you only
have ten units of suffering, not a hundred units.

Let's say you get very good at meditation and you learn to
meditate on the qualities of pain so you have close to zero

resistance to suffering. Then you may have a very intense pain but there is little or no suffering involved at all!

Now the practical consequence of this. Shinzen is aware this is a nice theory, but that theories have to be tested. He has now worked with a number of people who have chronic pain problems that can't be helped medically and he's taught them vipassana meditation, with special emphasis on his techniques for dealing with pain. Let's say that they have a chronic back pain problem that physicians can't do anything effective about. Shinzen will teach the sufferer focused varieties of vipassana, for example something like: "Okay, as you meditate tell me *exactly* where the pain is right now." The sufferer might say "It's from the bottom of my neck to half way down my back." Then Shinzen will say something like, "Let's take the *exact* location of that pain, moment by moment, as the object of your meditation. I want you to observe it carefully and follow any changes in location." After a few minutes Shinzen might ask something like "Okay, where is the pain now? Is it in the same place or has it moved?" and get an answer like "Well it goes further down my back now." Helping the sufferer (who is probably not suffering quite so much already) focus further, Shinzen would then ask something like "Okay, how far down your back?" He'd acknowledge the answer and remind the sufferer to keep following the exact location of the pain moment by moment.

Something very interesting happens as the sufferer does this. Somehow in getting into this directed observation, opening up to *exactly* where the pain is now, the resistance has gone down. The pain is still there but the person is not suffering as much.

Other qualities of the pain than bodily location could be used. Shinzen might ask them about qualities of the pain, for instance, and somebody might say it has a stabbing quality. "Okay, how stabbing? If you rated the stabbingness on a 7- point scale, how stabbing is it right now?" The sufferer/

meditator might rate it as a 5. And then later, "Okay, is it still stabbing at the same level, or more stabbing, or less stabbing? What is its rating?" Getting the sufferer to follow the intensity of the stabbing quality moment-by-moment, the resistance goes down because the meditator, instead of constantly saying to himself something like, "Oh my God, my pain, I don't deserve it, why does it happen to me? The world's unjust, I can't stand it!" is directing his attention to the process of tracking the intensity of the stabbing sensation. You all know how we can work ourselves up about these things! But this kind of conscious meditation changes things.

Shinzen has found that by getting people to take this meditative opening up attitude, practicing vipassana with qualities of the pain as the attentional focus, resistance goes down and the suffering cuts way back. He has worked with people who have chronic pain problems that opiates can't handle, but after teaching them this meditative procedure, the pain is still there, but somehow they're now able to function in life again, their degree of suffering goes way down.

Understand that I am giving you my crude understanding of Shinzen's work here. "Resistance," for example, is a multi-dimensional concept dealing with images, internal talk, reaction to these, etc. He hasn't written much yet but the material should become available soon on his website, www.shinzen.org.

So, we had a pain, right? We had a pain and it went away and I think one of the reasons it went away is because instead of our habitual attitude of resistance, of "Go away!" you took this open quality of mind toward it. And that made a difference.

STUDENT: *I have a mathematical problem with that. If your resistance drops to zero and you, uh . . .*

Your intellect is working overtime, isn't it?

(General laughter)

STUDENT: *If your resistance drops to zero and you look at your pain, your pain increases to infinity!*

No, that's not it. You're taking the equation form too literally but mixing the variables. Pain, as defined in this equation, is the actual physiological process. It's the actual rate of nerve firing caused by damage somewhere. Pain is not a psychological variable here: suffering is what's psychological.

STUDENT: *I was surprised at the many different things I experienced in my body during our practice, pain and good feelings, energy and numbness, many, many things. I was never so aware of so many different things in my body! Normally my body doesn't seem to have much sensation in it at all!*

That's good that you experienced all these things in your body. The truth is there is a lot going on in there, all the time. We've just shut the door on it. There is a lot going on in our bodies, and a lot of that constitutes our basic joy of being alive. It's like the "motors" are turning over, the juices and vital energies are flowing and all that, all the time, and when we cut our body out of awareness, we live in abstractions. If you go back to our analogy of your going to a friend's house to taste this marvelous concoction that she has made, it's as if what we usually do is we say, "Oh, just give me the recipe, I don't need to taste it." We're going to the restaurant of life and mostly just reading the menu in great detail instead of actually tasting and chewing the food. Not too nutritious!

STUDENT: *My experience is that it's not as relaxing or enjoyable to follow sensations all over my body as it is to focus on a single object, like in the breathing meditation.*

All right. Now there is an implicit assumption in what you said. The assumption is that the purpose of that meditation was to relax or enjoy yourself. That we meditate to feel good. You're not alone in that one! You have an attachment to getting something pleasant and worthwhile from the meditation. That's quite understandable.

Now, there is nothing wrong with wanting things in life, with having goals, with wanting to get something from things, and so forth. That's perfectly normal, perfectly natural, but —

most of the meditative traditions would say that, unfortunately, this "natural" desire has gotten so out of hand that it drives us nuts. We get too attached to the positive things and too averse to the negative ones and the result is living in illusion, in samsara.

In the concentrative meditation practice, for instance, there is an obvious goal — the goal to learn to focus better — although that goal is itself in the service of a higher purpose in the meditative traditions. So the goal of the meditative practice is something more than enjoying it. It tends to happen that the sensations from successful concentrative meditation are pleasurable, but that's not the main point. In fact, if you gradually start doing concentrative meditation in a way that makes it very pleasurable, you may actually find you're not concentrating properly anymore. You're concentrating on holding on to the pleasure, instead of on the designated focus of a particular meditation session. I'm not saying you're doing this, but it can easily slip over into that instead of trying to develop the basic concentrative ability.

The point of concentrative meditation, as I'm teaching it today, is to train your mind so that if you decide, for whatever reason, that you're going to have 99 percent of your attention focused on "A," whatever "A" is, you can do it, no matter what happens. Whether it's pleasurable or painful. You should be able to concentrate on a very unpleasant sensation with full intensity if you chose to do it. A reasonable ability in concentrative meditation (you don't have to hit the 99 percent level) then forms the basis of success in vipassana.

The point of the vipassana meditation — the opening up meditation — is that instead of concentrating on one thing, we will observe the full play of experience, with clarity. We decide that instead of constantly manipulating our experience, which we're doing all the time, we want to see what it really is without interfering with it, without having it hidden behind conceptual and manipulative screens. To put this back in the essential science terms we began with today, we have an inkling that we've gotten lost in theories that are misleading us in important ways, so we are trying to develop a method for really getting a clearer perception and understanding of the actual data, reality, rather than theory acting as blind, automatized beliefs which distort our perceptions. This becomes clearer and clearer as you learn these techniques.

We are 110 percent manipulators, working over our flow of experience every microsecond, trying to make pleasant things better or get rid of what we don't like.

Now there is nothing wrong with wanting to do that up to a "reasonable" degree, but when it's compulsive, automatized, when, in a sense, you can never allow yourself to experience what's happening without controlling it, you're living in a restricted portion of the spectrum of the whole possibility of life. So what vipassana meditation practice really aims at doing is opening us up to clear perception of what's actually happening at the moment.

Now in terms of how "good" a given meditation is, a vipassana meditation session where you really stayed strongly in contact with an unpleasant sensation for a long period of time, without being distracted for long, is, in a real sense, a much greater accomplishment than if you drifted off into something nice and pleasant and didn't notice what was going on. Remember, your goal had been to pay attention to the natural flow, and if instead you drifted off into something that was pleasant but partially "created," not the "natural" flow, you didn't do it. But again recognize also that there is a lot of variability when you're first beginning this, and even when you get very good at it.

One of the ways people get stuck in any kind of meditation practice is that they have some experience during the meditation session that's rewarding and they think "Aha! Now I've finally got it!" Then they consciously forget the actual instructions for the meditation practice and simply try to reproduce the experience that was rewarding before. We've touched on this before. Now I can't blame people for that. I do it all the time myself! But if I want to learn to be able to concentrate whenever and wherever I wish to, and all I learn is to concentrate on things I happen to like, that's not so good. It's already easy to concentrate on (to be *passively concentrated on*, to put it more accurately) things that you like.

STUDENT: *You use the "C" word, the control word.*

The "C" word — the control word. I like that phrasing. Okay. Is control politically incorrect now? *(laughter)*

STUDENT: *No, no, it's correct. So Shinzen Young has the people observe the pain. Sometimes they observe that the pain goes up, or the pain goes down, the suffering going up, the suffering going down: people now know that they control it. Milton Erickson, the hypnotherapist, even encouraged people to increase the pain. That's one way to show people they have control. So what's your perspective on that control process? Is this control good? This is a Western perspective, I guess.*

Yes, it's definitely a Western perspective. It's all right to have a Western perspective: we are Westerners!

As to control — the formal instructions in vipassana meditation are to fully experience, open mindedly, whatever sensation comes along moment by moment, without attempting to control what the sensation is or becomes. Without trying to amplify the good or inhibit the bad, and so forth. That sounds in many ways like an injunction to *not* control, but, of course, it does contain the injunction to control your attention, to keep paying attention and not drift off the way we usually drift off or let habitual patterns of craving and aversion manipulate your attention and your experience. So there is a balance here, okay? I would not say that meditative traditions are about exerting no control whatsoever. At some of the very highest levels you get into something like that. But meanwhile, you obviously have to decide you're going to sit down and have a meditation session. You're going to have a purpose for the meditation session. If you're doing it to deal with chronic pain, you may, in a sense, be trying to stop the usual controlling mechanisms in order to focus clearly on some aspect of the pain, but in the background is indeed an implicit desire to control the nature of this experience.

STUDENT: *There was a big difference in the two kinds of meditation for me. I liked the concentrative meditation, I really settled into a lovely kind of peace. Yet in a way it was sort of dull compared to the other kind, where a whole bunch of interesting sensations happened. I wondered if I should exert any control over it, though, whether it would be natural to control meditation.*

So concentrative meditation is peaceful for you and vipassana is more interesting? I suspect the control issue is partly a pseudo issue here, because I don't think we realize what control freaks we already are. It's not as if we're introducing some control where there was no control before; we're modifying the focus of various kinds of controls that we try to exercise all the time, and we're trying to make the control process more conscious. All of the meditative traditions would say you're constantly attempting to control experience as well as being controlled by a million factors all the time that affect the way the run of your thoughts goes.

Here, let's bring the control dimension up to a more conscious level by trying to exert some deliberate control and seeing what we can learn from this. Including learning how little conscious control we have! Again, I go back to that example I mentioned before that a lot of people who try concentrative meditation say, "This is awful, it makes my thoughts race like mad!" Well that's just the way it is naturally, our thoughts are always racing.

Now we've been getting a little too intellectual. I want us to try ten minutes more of vipassana before we get off into too many concepts here. If you'll excuse my implicitly using the "C" word in exerting control! You guys are such good thoughtaholics, I really have to discipline myself not to be tempted to have a few more conceptual drinks myself!

Okay. So let's try vipassana, opening up meditation for ten minutes. I'll walk you through it again.

(The following exercise should be spread over about ten minutes — or longer when you get comfortable with it)

Sit in a comfortable posture . . .

Either close your eyes . . . or park them comfortably on some convenient spot in front of you . . .

Bring your attention into your body sensations . . . and start opening your mind to paying attention, open minded attention, to whatever the strongest bodily sensation at the moment is . . . Open your mind to experiencing it . . . like you've never felt this sensation before . . .

What is it? The *words* that come in response to the attitude of curiosity don't matter . . . it's being aware of what the *qualities* of sensation are at this very moment . . .

And at *this* very moment? . . .

And at *this* very moment? . . .

Beware the tendency of your mind to put a verbal label on it and then stop actually paying attention . . . because reality keeps changing, even though your label implies permanence, implies that you know all about this sensation and don't have to pay attention any longer . . .

So what's that sensation at *this* moment?

Now remember, if your mind has drifted off into thinking about things, just *gently* come back to sense whatever the strongest sensation of the moment is . . . What are you sensing at *this* moment?

If words get automatically attached to sensations, just let that be secondary . . . Keep focusing back on the actual quality of sensation . . .

Our minds tend to classify things and then say in effect, "I've seen this before, no point in paying further attention."

Keep coming back to the actual quality of the sensation at each moment . . . Maybe it's the same — maybe it's not . . .

Now in a minute I'm going to suggest we finish this practice . . . but before we do, take the focus of your attention now and instead of focusing it on internal body sensations, bring it to your hearing . . .

Notice the quality of the room sound-wise, or any sounds there might be . . .

And now split your attention, so you have some general awareness of your body, but keep being aware of the sound qualities of the room . . . or any sounds reaching your ears . . . There is nothing you should or shouldn't experience, just try to be aware of what's going on in your experience at the moment as you stay aware of your body and aware of whatever sounds you're hearing . . .

Okay. Now open your eyes if they're closed, and bring your style of mental functioning back to what passes for normal.

(Several hands go up, indicating eager questions.)

You guys really are a temptation! You're all full of these interesting ideas and questions, and you really seriously tempt the thoughtaholic in me to lots of discussion, but I'm going to be very disciplined in insisting we keep coming back to giving you a taste of how to do these practices. A proper meditation teacher would start you practicing again instead of being tempted by all those hands waving!

But since we only have a few minutes left before our lunch break, and I'm not very proper, we'll give in for now and indulge that part of your mind that really is full of all these interesting questions and ideas and desperately wants to know. Try to keep your questions close to experience if you can, though. Don't worry that you're not going to get enough intellectual stimulation! Remember, we have an intellectual orgy coming up for all the week at this conference!

STUDENT: *I had an experience here. I thought you said something about an alternative to paying attention to sensation would be paying attention to thinking? That seemed to work a lot better for me. Could you tell me something about that?*

So paying attention to your thinking works better for you?

STUDENT: *Yes, I was noticing something about what I forgot to do before I came here. I was thinking about what I'm going to do when I leave here and thinking about what you said earlier, thinking about what I wanted to say to you earlier.*

That sounds like normal consciousness!

STUDENT: *Well, the thing was I don't normally notice this kind of thought.*

You may be one of the lucky ones who can begin observing thought relatively soon in a meditative practice. What I said earlier was that observing thought is a very difficult way for most people to begin to learn to meditate; it's tricky and difficult to try to observe our thought processes because the thought processes tend to absorb all our attention and run on in almost endless chains. To keep that little "split," to keep a part of you observing what's going on, is easier with body sensations.

So returning to your question: what are you asking about your body as you start thinking?

STUDENT: *It gets ignored.*

It gets ignored. Remember again this working model I find so useful, namely that we only have so much attention available and the intellect can gobble it all up. There is nothing left for sensation, you know. Until something as intense as a fire engine comes by, you hardly notice anything's happening — and that's "normal" — and it lets most of the joy go out of life.

Too much of life is like that. You walk by a rose bush and don't notice it at all. Occasionally you remember that you've been told to stop and smell the roses, so you stop for a fraction of a second on your busy rounds and mentally say to yourself, "Smells nice — nice roses." But what you've really smelled is mostly your ideas about roses, and what you've really looked at is your concepts about roses. Now, this is very hard to convey, especially in an intellectual manner, but, believe me, there is a great richness possible to life if you learn to stop and come to your senses. I'm going to focus a lot on that this afternoon. It is really gratifying. But it only happens if we stop being trapped in our intellect. Intellect is a wonderful tool, but it's a terrible master.

STUDENT: *I'm trying to figure out whether ringing in the ears is a body sensation.*

Ringing in the ears a body sensation? Well most of us would say it was a sound. Unless there is a specific body component to it; if you feel a tactile quality to it also, then sure.

Now again, you can get too caught up in doing meditation practice exactly right. You know, is this *really* a body sensation? Much of the time I've wasted trying to learn how to meditate was because I wanted to do it exactly right. I once had a teacher of awareness in everyday life (our afternoon topic) who said his main job with his students was to teach us to lower our standards! Things got much better for me after I took that advice seriously! If it's a prominent sensation that comes in during practice like this, sure, check it out as long as it's there. But don't get too lost in the issue of whether it is really a body sensation or not.

STUDENT: *There seems to be a moment of sensation that corresponds to one of the senses, like tactile. Seems like most of what you've been asking us to do is tactile awareness. And I noticed during the breathing focus that I couldn't get rid of an auditory correlate of that. It wasn't a real sound, but while I was paying attention to the in and out of breathing I had this quality of sound. Is there kind of a sensory modality of awareness that you're talking about? As a correlate?*

If you got very good at this opening up meditation, you would begin paying attention to the full simultaneous sensory spectrum, opening up to the whole flow of experience. Okay. And it turns out all sorts of things are associated at the experiential level that we may hold completely separate at the everyday conceptual level. For instance, one of the things I found is when I'm doing vipassana well, just about every sound that comes along has a very specific effect somewhere in my body. Each creates a very specific sensation at some particular location in my body. It amazed me when I started to observe this; I thought hearing took place in the ear!

I'll give you an exercise you can all do over lunch time if you want to stretch your minds a little bit, instead of just having a good intellectual time. *Listen to whatever sounds there are with your feet.* Drop the preconception that hearing takes place in your ear. Listen with your feet. Feel the sensations in your feet as people say things, as you hear various sounds and so forth. Yes! It sounds crazy, right. Your intellect will say that sounds crazy; I can't do that — but try it.

Okay. I'm going to end this now so we can get some lunch. We'll start officially again at 1:15.

CHAPTER 6

Links, Expansions, Concepts

I've always found that people are not ready for focused work right after the lunch breaks at a workshop, so we can have a few minutes of general discussion about what we've been doing, before we get involved with mindfulness in everyday life. There are always a few people late getting back from lunch, too!

STUDENT: *Talking with people over lunch, some of us found the concentrative meditation practice easier and more rewarding, for others it was the vipassana practice. What causes these differences?*

I don't have the slightest idea what brings these differences about when you start to learn meditation, but they happen. There is no standard psychological textbook I can now look in and say, "Oh! She's one of such-and-such a type of person if she liked concentrative meditation more." Probably there is something in classical Buddhist literature about this — there is an enormous amount of scholarly writing, as well as practice tradition, in Buddhism, but I'm no scholar of Buddhism.

But, at the data level, the observational level, there is enormous individual variation in how people react to meditation. I've tried to make some general statements in introducing meditation, statement that are likely to be helpful to almost everyone, but what's right on and "true" for one person may not at all be "true" or particularly helpful for another person at this stage of our Western knowledge of meditation.

What's a scientist like me doing teaching an exotic technique like meditation, anyway? One of the reasons I've started doing it instead of sticking to just doing research in more concrete areas is that I think what we currently know of meditation in the West is very useful for helping people in many ways, but the basic principles need to be put into a form that makes more sense in our culture. People hear about some ancient technique. It's venerable and all that, but does it work today? If you were, say, a 13th-century Persian, an ancient Persian meditation technique might have been just the thing for most 13th-century Persians, but the words don't have the same connotations anymore. We're 20th-century Westerners; the techniques don't have the same effect. By teaching meditation, I'm both experimenting with learning more about it myself and I'm seeing what sorts of ways of expressing it are useful, are pedagogically effective.

Let me say something about meditation techniques in general. This is something I usually make a point about when I'm trying to explain altered states of consciousness (ASCs) and I talk about induction techniques for inducing particular ASCs (see, e.g., (Tart 1975)). You can look at the details of any induction technique, but if you don't know the context — the personal, and social expectational context in which an induction technique is carried out — you have little idea of what's going to happen as a result of applying it. To illustrate this, I often show people one of the world's most powerful techniques for inducing an altered state of consciousness. Look. You take a piece of chalk and draw a circle — and keep going around and around and around, tracing the circle over and over again (*illustrates*). For hours if necessary. If you're an Eskimo shaman, this is a very powerful technique for going into an altered state where you can experience speaking to the spirits. Without that expectation, it's mainly a way of getting bored.

It's the same principle now with meditation. I've given you primarily the essence of two major techniques, but they're always used in a context, and the context that these techniques are used in can make big differences in exactly how they are used and what's liable to result from using them. If we were in a Buddhist culture, for instance, and you had been raised on Buddhism since you were infants, I wouldn't have to mention things like this is "designed to produce enlightenment," or this will overcome your "poisonous cravings," or things like that. All that would feed in implicitly, and it would give your understanding and use of the techniques a certain flavor.

Now I'm trying to adapt to our "local culture" today. It's the culture of people who come to a conference on the scientific study of consciousness, a culture which is genuinely scientific in an important sense. Yes, I suspect most of you are a bunch of closet "spiritual seekers" too, since we're human, but we're playing scientists this particular week. But also I've adapted to that local culture context, because meditation makes a lot of sense in the Tucson III context of trying to develop a science of consciousness. So I guess that there are many underlying assumptions I've been influenced by and influenced you with in the presentations I've given and will give today. I have an assumption, for example, that people here are curious about the way the mind works. I have another assumption that people wouldn't mind creating a little better quality of personal life, or that people here believe we can learn things from other people. I have an assumption that civilization is making progress, that we can learn to know more than people in older times did. Those are aspects of the "local culture" we're working in that influence what I say and do, and that influence how you hear, perceive and interpret what we do.

STUDENT: *How do you locate meditation within the framework of altered states in general? If altered states are up here* (gestures high) *and ordinary consciousness is down here* (gestures low), *where among the altered states is meditation?*

Ah! Well first, I don't necessarily put altered states "up here," above ordinary consciousness. In my scientific approach to ASCs, I'm very careful to use the term "altered state of consciousness" only descriptively, in a value-free way (Tart 1975). ASC is a general description for a radically different style of mental functioning, and there are a number of ASCs. A particular ASC may be much better for some things and much worse for other things, compared to ordinary consciousness or other ASCs, but I don't intend any blanket implication of "higher" or "lower" when I describe a state as an ASC. It's just significantly *different*. What a particular ASC is "better" for or "worse" for is something to discover empirically, not have *a priori* judgments about.

Sometimes meditation practices can produce ASCs, especially if that's the expectational context you bring to it. Or you can drop that ASC context entirely and say meditation training is primarily about "purifying" your ordinary state of consciousness, the place where you normally live. Remember our example of the Zen student who saw the gods and goddesses bowing down to him? Sounds like an ASC experience to me, but his master considered it a distraction and reminded him to keep track of his breathing.

So, in our ordinary state of consciousness, to roughly characterize it, we have a zillion thoughts and associated emotions an hour, largely controlled by habit and earlier social conditioning history (constituting *you*, your "personality"). There is little real freedom in ordinary consciousness. If we had real freedom and someone said, "Look at that painting over there, see its visual details, and think of nothing else for the next hour," we could do it. Real, practical freedom would involve powerful, if not perfect, control over how we used our own minds. But we can't do something like that. Our minds are largely out of our control, and the patterns of uncontrolled thought and feeling in our minds are largely conditioned. We have very little freedom. And it's called being "normal."

Now, if I may personify the culture for the sake of making a point, the culture doesn't want us to know how little real freedom we have because, given the particular way we're conditioned, we'll lust after and buy more goods and so increase the gross national product, which theoretically will make us all happier, or something like that. It does indeed sound like a gross national product to me! So I'm teaching meditation (and the mindfulness training we will shortly come to) primarily within this context of purifying ordinary consciousness, rather than as a way of inducing ASCs. This is my "bias," and I want you to know it.

If I were the kind of person who got into all sorts of blissful ASCs when I meditated, I'd probably think of it more that way. Certainly some teachers think of meditation that way. But I'm not. I'm a very down to earth and practical person in spite of — because of? —"far out" interests like ASCs.

So the way I'm presenting meditation and mindfulness to you is based on the idea of "purifying" ordinary consciousness, of learning to focus where you want, and then starting to have greater openness to your basic experience, to have "insights." I use insights in this context mainly in the psychological sense now of a much deeper understanding of who you really are, and what your nature is. Gaining such openings and insights should slowly lead, in my experience, to a progressive transformation of your ordinary consciousness.

The basic vipassana meditation I've taught you, paying attention to the flow of body sensations, should not be underrated: I'm told that's what Gotama Siddhartha was practicing when he became enlightened, when he became the Buddha. (Note that "Buddha" is not a personal name, it's a technical term to characterize people who have reached the highest level of enlightenment.) So the practice comes with a pretty good pedigree! He practiced a few other techniques also (to put it mildly!), but vipassana meditation, if taken to a high enough degree of perfection, is supposed to be incredibly transformative.

Now I sometimes claim that my expertise is not on enlightenment but on *endarkenment!* I believe I'm far, far away from whatever enlightenment is, so I don't personally know how far the vipassana process can take you. But I do know from my own experience (and that of friends) that by learning to tune into your body and into current, ongoing reality with clearer attention, by learning to discriminate actual, immediate experience from abstractions and theories and reactions about reality, an important change gradually takes place. Then, rather than usually being stuck in your thoughts, you become a more intelligent and perceptive person, and life becomes much more satisfactory.

Returning to your question more directly: my emphasis is that meditation practices *per se* are much more important for training and purifying all aspects of consciousness than experiencing any particular altered state. There are technical Buddhist works that classify different altered states which may be arrived at by meditative practices, but most of those states are beyond my understanding, so I won't speculate about them.

STUDENT: *Would you find the results of a dream while you are meditating, like going to sleep, or being asleep and dreaming? I'm having very real experiences here.*

Tell me more about what you mean. "Dream" is a very broad word.

STUDENT: *Sometimes as we've practiced meditating here I've found I've suddenly gone off into a dream.*

By dreaming, you mean you're seeing things, doing things in an inner world of experience, there is a plot?

STUDENT: *Yes.*

Is it as vivid as nighttime dreaming is for you?

STUDENT: *Yes.*

You're probably dropping down into the hypnagogic state, which lets that dreamlike activity go on. It's quite normal. Strictly speaking, traditionally speaking, it's one more distraction from actually doing the meditation practice.

The speed of distraction continues to amaze me! After a number of years of practicing meditation, I can sometimes, for moments, get really clear and present to reality. When I'm in that kind of state, that ASC, it's obviously the only sensible way to exist. I realize I've been dreaming my life away, I've now (at least partially) awakened, and this clarity, presence and awakeness is a much more satisfying and sensible place to live life from. And then, to my (later) utter amazement, within a fraction of a second, instantaneously as far as psychological time is concerned, I'm in a complete other world of existence. One of these other worlds is called normal consciousness, with my concerns and my plans and my hopes and fears and considerations and theories. Or I've slipped into another world of the hypnagogic state: that whole world, with its sights, sounds, actions and plots has come into existence, bang! Just like that!

These kinds of transitions happens all the time to lots of people. You're probably slipping in and out of the hypnagogic state when that happens, given what you've said. As I've said about other kinds of distraction people have reported, don't beat yourself up about it! It happens. But if you're trying to focus on your breath, when you realize it's happened, gently come back to the breath. If you're trying to keep track of the whole flow of body sensations, gently come back to the whole flow of body sensations. If you're trying to keep track of the most prominent body sensation, gently come back to the most prominent body sensation.

The Tibetans have a rather good attitude about unusual experiences as distractions, I think. They say meditation practices may lead you to extraordinary experiences once in a while (*nyams* in Tibetan, *makyo* in Zen), and that's fine: then just get back to the meditation practice. Experiences are experiences are experiences. Don't get too carried away by them. Don't make a big deal out of them. They change, like everything else. They're impermanent.

One final conceptual note: someone asked me during the break, "Isn't it dangerous to teach these practices out of context?" Put in extreme form, "Shouldn't you be in a monastery or nunnery before you're trained in them?"

Meditation is "dangerous," in one sense. If you teach psychotics, really unstable people, how to meditate, they'll probably get worse. I'm making the assumption that, since nobody here has their keeper with them, you're all "normal." You're all allowed to walk around loose, so I assume that you're all intelligent enough to try the techniques and, if you like them and results are good, you'll keep them up. If they cause major disturbances, you'll stop, and either get some help on what already existing psychological problems have been aggravated by the meditation and/or get help from a qualified meditation teacher on how to practice in a way that's growthful but not disturbing.

But let's think a little more deeply about the question of whether it's dangerous to teach something like this. When we shift from the isolated question to think about it in the context of modern life, the question of whether practicing meditation is "dangerous" is not really the relevant question. Life is already dangerous! We see similar isolated questions all the time. Is this drug dangerous? Is this procedure dangerous? Is being hypnotized dangerous? As if we were normally perfectly safe and were thinking of adding something to this safe life that might be dangerous. *We're not safe!* In "normal" life we have enormous numbers of suicides, for instance, both obvious suicides and people working themselves to death. We have enormous cruelty. I don't have to tell you what a sad state the world is in. We're in pretty bad shape to begin with.

So the relevant question is, "What are the relative possible pluses and minuses, advantages and disadvantages, gains and losses for beginning a meditation practice, given the current situation of a given person in their world today?" For some, such as our hypothetical psychotic, the minuses, the likely increase in symptoms, will probably outweigh any possible pluses. For others, like some of us, what might be dangerous would be to just let things go on as they are, to not start meditation or mindfulness practices in our lives! I wish we had really reliable ways of predicting the likelihood of various plusses and minuses, but we don't. We don't know enough.

CHAPTER 7

Self-Observation & Self-Remembering in Everyday Life

If you regularly practice the two meditation techniques I've given you this morning, hopefully under at least occasional direction of a skilled meditation teacher, you could produce some major changes in your life. Traditionally, you're supposed to practice only concentrative meditation for a long time without bothering with insight meditation. You're supposed to do that till you reach a certain level of proficiency, technically called *access concentration*, which basically means you can pretty much keep your mind on what you intend to for long periods of time. But in modern times, the two kinds of meditation are usually taught together and, of course, vipassana meditation clearly involves concentration. You have to monitor what's going on and keep your mind focused to a specified range of ongoing sensations. But if you practiced just these two things, most of you could easily — by easily, I mean for most people within a few months, for some people much sooner than that — develop a routine where you could sit down for fifteen minutes or twenty minutes a day, have your body go into a very relaxed state, have your mind get much calmer than normal, and have a fair amount of the stress of the day, accumulated up to that point, release itself.

This would happen because one of the things that opening up meditation, vipassana meditation, does, is that when you attend to body sensations, previously unconscious tensions are liable to come up into conscious awareness. When a tension comes up as a sensation, your instructions are not to reject it or fight it, but to be open to it and pay clear attention to it, taste its flavor as it were — but as you do this, most tensions tend to then automatically relax. It's like if you know you're walking around like this (CTT *takes very tense, shoulders up high posture, and walks around*), it's a very stupid thing to do, and you're naturally going to relax out of it! If you have very little contact with your body, though, you may create and hold this kind of tension all day long. You steadily accumulate tensions, which I'm sure are very bad for your health in general. So vipassana meditation and/or concentrative meditation (or a combination of them) would indeed give you a routine where you can sit down once or twice a day for a few minutes, relax the body, relax the mind a lot more — and have insights come along.

Now, I've been cagey about using this word "insight," because I don't want to mean it just in the psychological sense. Let's say you would probably have clearer perceptions of aspects of what you do, who you are, how your habitual patterns work and so forth — and in some cases, simply having those insights will change you. When you realize you've been doing something very stupid, a lot of times that's sufficient. Other times you have to hang in there and keep on clearly perceiving things you may not like at all.

When I began practicing mindfulness in life, for example, I really became aware of the attitude I'd long had toward people who tailgate me on the freeway. I wanted to kill the

#*$#@!! bastards for threatening my life, and they deserved to die!!! I was amazed at the intensity of this feeling. I think of myself as a mild mannered professor, but I really wanted those people to get their just deserts, to die for threatening me with their stupid behavior.

I had begun a serious mindfulness in life practice of the sort we'll be discussing soon, though, so I was committed to clearly and fully seeing what was, and I hung in there. The parts of my mind I preferred to think of as "me" didn't like seeing this intense desire to kill, but I figured it would come up a few times, I'd keep looking at it, have my insight, and it would soon go away.

Nope! *Three years* of watching that desire to kill come up almost every day! Of course, in reality, my life was being threatened by a bunch of idiots who weren't keeping a proper and safe following distance, so I suppose this reality had something to do with keeping the feeling so strong, but there was little or nothing I could do about their behavior. Slamming on my brakes when someone is tailgating is also dangerous in reality and doesn't seem to educate anyone to drive better. My reaction, which was causing me pain, was something I could possibly control, through insight and mindfulness. Well, eventually the repeated observation of this reaction with clarity and some equanimity did diminish it — although I still don't like tailgaters in reality!

I've kept our discussions and practice in a simple context today, and the choice is up to you as to how much of these meditational techniques you want to bring into your life, how much you want to practice by yourself and/or whether you want to get even better at it by getting expert coaching from some local (where you live) meditation teacher who could help you. But with these practices you have here the possibilities of something that could make a major difference in your life, as well as helping provide the skills for a science of consciousness.

When the Eastern spiritual traditions speak of living in a state of illusion, in maya, in samsara, and that living in illusion is what is called "normal" by everyday standards — it makes, sadly, perfect sense to me. The funny thing to me has always been that the idea of "living in illusion" sounds very strange for Westerners: we don't have that concept. But if you look at what we know about psychology and psychiatry, you would find that we know far more about the actual mechanics of living in illusion than I think they do in the East! We know dozens of ways in which you can distort your perception of reality, and have all sorts of crazy defense mechanisms, distortions of perception and judgment, neuroses, and so forth. We just don't put it together to see how much we live in illusion, because after all, we're "normal," therefore we don't apply that knowledge to ourselves.

So now for bringing today's meditative focus into everyday life.

I presume nobody here particularly wants to withdraw from life and sit on a cushion for eight or more hours a day and just meditate, that most of us want to continue on with ordinary life. Ordinary life can be a drag, but ordinary life can also be a lot of fun and a real challenge! So, let's say you're talking with a coworker who says something that pushes one of your emotional buttons. You get pretty absorbed in chains of internal thoughts and emotions. Then you no longer hear much of anything that your coworker says because you're seething inside at the imagined slight. It can get worse for, caught in this internal loop, your perception becomes distorted and you misinterpret what little you do hear of your coworker's words to find further aggravation in them. Your coworker may not have intended any hurt, the perceived threat may be a distortion on your part.

There is far too much of this in ordinary life. Wouldn't it be nice if you could do something like this meditation then? If you could, in some sense, listen to the actual sound of your coworker's voice, instead of the annoying whine your psychological defense mechanisms have changed it into? Hear the actual words your co-worker speaks, before all these samsaric reactions get piled on top of them and destroy the original meaning of the words and whatever their sense was? Might we not have a chance to act and react much more adaptively, intelligently, and compassionately, if we kept in touch with reality, instead of getting lost in our emotional, samsaric reactions?

This afternoon I'm going to focus mainly on a technique for doing just that. This is a technique that is sometimes called *self-observation*, sometimes *self-remembering* (there are distinctions, but they needn't concern us today), and it's a technique for developing and practicing much greater mindfulness in everyday life.

I learned this primarily through the teachings of a man named G. I. Gurdjieff, who was one of the early pioneers in taking Eastern ideas of spiritual development and recasting them in forms that made sense to and were effective for modern Westerners. Instead of "This is the Holy and Venerable Practice done by Sufis 1600 years ago in Afghanistan, do it exactly the same way!" he taught something modern Westerners can do. I have adapted Gurdjieff's methods and ideas in various ways, linking them with my knowledge of modern psychology. In case anybody is prone to make the mistake of projecting too much authority on to me as we get into this material, please note that I'm not an official member or representative of any organized Gurdjieff tradition or teaching lineage, and I'm certainly not "authorized" to teach anything by any of these "official" traditions, so all the mischief I do is my own responsibility. Fortunately! Well, actually one of my teachers in that tradition encouraged me to teach, but whether that is "official" or not is a complex political story, and I prefer to be non-official!

Gurdjieff had his own version of the concept of living in illusion, in samsara or maya. He put it both simply and in a number of ways. For one thing, he said that if you want to understand people, there is no point in studying psychology. Psychology is for real people. To study ordinary people, you study mechanics. He was clearly not trying to win friends and influence people! His primary way of putting it, repeated over and over again, is that "Man is asleep." To put it more technically, you might say that our ordinary state of consciousness is so dreamlike, is so much a pathologically distorted perception of what's really going on, both in terms of perceiving the real world around us and perceiving our own real nature, that it's like a dream.

Comparing ordinary consciousness, "normal" consciousness, to a dream is quite useful. When you're in a dream, you take it as real. Yes, I know about lucid dreams (which are still dreams), but we'll forget lucid dreams for now. In an ordinary dream, you take what's happening as being real while it's going on. You may get into all sorts of difficulties in the dream, suffer intense, unpleasant emotions and stress — but then you wake up, and all your problems are gone! You don't have to solve this terrible dream problem anymore, because it was just a dream! It wasn't really a problem in reality, it was a problem only in a state of illusion.

Gurdjieff said there is another awakening possible for human beings, an awakening from the sleep of ordinary consciousness. From the so-called awake state of ordinary consciousness — he thought it was a cruel joke to call ordinary consciousness a "waking" state, a "conscious" state — we could move into a genuinely awake state. From the perspective of this truly awakened state, ordinary consciousness could be seen as obviously very dreamlike, as a very distorted, feverish, crazy, driven state where we get into a lot of trouble and so suffer a lot, but suffer *uselessly.*

Gurdjieff noted that a fine thing about ordinary, nighttime sleep dreams is that no matter what you do in them, once you wake up, the consequences are gone. You can sign a check giving away all your savings in your nighttime dreams, but when you wake up, no problem. The trouble is we're really very badly out of it in our ordinary waking state — and we can sign checks, and the bank cashes them. So we live our life and act from a distorted state, waking sleep, samsara, maya.

Very relevant to the fact that we're at a scientific conference on developing a science of consciousness, Gurdjieff also had what I consider an essentially scientific attitude. Which is similar to what the Buddha had, actually. Both of them said, in effect, "I don't expect you to *believe* a word of what I teach. Especially once I'm gone, and have been made into some kind of spiritual authority! Do not accept any of what I've taught because it comes on authority, because other people believe in it, because it's venerable and what not. Take this stuff, give it enough initial energy or belief to activate it, and *test it*! If it works for you when you test it out, continue to work with it and use it. If it doesn't pass the test of working in the real world, don't believe a word of it!"

I like both Gurdjieff's and the Buddha's attitudes. Of course you know what happened with the Buddha for too many people: it's much easier to deify someone, worship them, and assume they will do the job of saving you than to actually go through all the work of practicing their teachings. A small proportion of people labeled (by us) as "Buddhists" actually do the meditations and other practices to check out Buddhism for themselves, and a small number of people actually do what Gurdjieff taught.

Gurdjieff told people they have to first become aware of the nature of the ordinary state they live in. The primary technique for this was self-observation. It was not sufficient to accept his statements that ordinary consciousness is dreamlike and distorted. You have to find this out for yourself. To do this, you do not engage in more intellectual analysis. We're already good at that. We've admitted that. Remember I started this workshop by stating that you all had world-class intellects? To really understand the nature of ordinary consciousness you have to, in a rather literal sense, go back to the data of life.

I talked about essential science this morning. My version of Gurdjieff's ideas is essential science applied on the level of psychological (dare I say "spiritual" in this group?) growth. Before you can change yourself in any really effective way, you have to get the data about how you really are. You have to make innumerable observations of what you're really like. What this usually means is years of trying to get in the habit of observing yourself, observing yourself in every possible situation, and observing yourself accurately, in detail, and impartially, as a scientist should. We have to develop an "observing function," and "observer."

Now most of us already have one kind of observer built in. Some people seem to lack it, but most of us have one that Freud called the *superego*. The superego is the fragmented part of ourselves that knows all the rules and is ready to judge us when we're bad. That's not a scientific observer, not an impartial, objective observer only curious to know the truth of things! That's an observer with a stake in things being the right way, an observer that is also a judge, jury, guard and executioner, an automated set of mental habits which has the ability to make us feel bad, feel guilty when we do something that it doesn't approve of. Gurdjieff had no use for the superego at all. It's a useful social mechanism for controlling the behavior of sleeping people, but otherwise it's not very good if you really want to wake up. You need to develop a much more scientific observer. You need to develop a portion of your mind that is curious about what am I *really* like? What do I *really* do? And to try to observe your external actions, your internal thoughts, your internal feelings and actions as clearly and objectively as possible.

Gurdjieff often used the analogy of developing a part of yourself that could take mental snapshots, gradually building up a huge album of such snapshots of what you're actually like in all sorts of situations in life. That was back when photographs didn't lie! Before we had digital retouching available, so of course the analogy leaves something to be desired nowadays. But Gurdjieff's approach really is a fundamentally scientific attitude. What are you really like when you're at the store talking to the clerk, when you're on the toilet, when you're teaching a class, when you're in the laboratory? As you collect numerous snapshots and develop and perfect a commitment to looking at them as objectively as possible, to see what you're really like, the foundation for effective growth is laid.

That attitude of observing yourself, of creating a neutral observer, a *fair witness*, as it's sometimes been called, is a major mental discipline in and of itself that will begin to bring about major changes in you. Gurdjieff presented it as a rather passive data gathering process, paired with the injunction to try not to change yourself for the first few years of self-observation practice. If you try to change yourself before you really understand yourself, you'll probably cause trouble. I've got some wrenches and screwdrivers, for instance; anybody need their car tuned up? I don't actually know much about how engines work, but I could loosen and tighten some things and take off some parts whose function doesn't make sense to me. I suspect you wouldn't really want me to work on your car!

Gurdjieff thought that most attempts at self change — most if not all of the world's self-improvement systems — were liable not to work well because they were done without a clear understanding of exactly how one's own mental machinery worked. So first you have to build up a fund of understanding from all these mental snapshots. You do that by using what little control over attention you have to create a part that watches, that observes. That observing part ideally doesn't approve or disapprove of what it sees, it usually doesn't try to interfere, but it just tries to get the facts. To get clearer perception of what *is*, without confusing it with what we've been taught *should* be.

Sounds a lot like vipassana meditation, doesn't it? You can certainly describe vipassana meditation that way, as a method of trying to take a part of the mind and devote it to just getting clearer perceptions of what actually is happening moment to moment. The big, obvious difference here between the traditional vipassana approach and Gurdjieff's approach is that vipassana is largely done sitting on a cushion in a quiet room, because, technically speaking, it's very helpful to meditate under those kind of conditions. You are cutting down outside distractions, so you're more likely to notice the workings of your own mind and your own body and learn important things that way. Gurdjieff thought that going off on a special spiritual practice retreat once in a while might indeed be a useful technical maneuver, but it only has limited value because the place you generate all your troubles is in everyday life. So the place you really need to see what you're really like, to be mindful, is in everyday life. That's where the action is.

It can be pretty easy (ignoring how hard learning meditation is for some people) to be "peaceful" and "spiritual" and "compassionate" if you're off in a beautiful place, sitting with a bunch of happy looking and like-minded people who are also sitting on their cushions, contemplating the beauty of the trees and flowers. We can all feel pretty good in pleasant circumstances. Not like when that #$%%*#! bastard cuts you off on the freeway, or tailgates too close behind you! So Gurdjieff emphasized the absolute necessity of developing mindfulness, "waking up," in everyday life.

While self-observation is a technique to practice by yourself in all aspects of your life, there are social assistance/reinforcement and special assisted circumstances. Students come to regular group meetings, for instance, and talk about things they have observed about themselves as a result of working on being more mindful in their lives, and so get a certain amount of social support for their efforts, as well as technical pointers from the teacher and more experienced students. This helps, of course, a great deal. It's very hard to do mindfulness practice with no social support whatsoever, to be the only one around who is interested in this kind of thing. Mindfulness, trying to observe the truth of what is in spite of what it's supposed to be, is not exactly a major social goal in our culture.

People learn a lot about themselves doing Gurdjieffian self-observation. I'll talk about the techniques for doing this shortly. Everyone, for instance, will learn about parts of themselves which they do not like, which they are embarrassed to discover! We all have parts of ourselves like that. People will also learn about parts of themselves that are really quite wonderful but which are also highly suppressed. "I'm a tough guy; I don't coddle people like some wimp — but I notice that I'm actually quite gentle with people who are hurting," or something like that. So there are a whole variety of things to observe, not just negative aspects of our selves. A lot of positive things get repressed, as well as negative things, under the pressures of our social system.

So this is self-observation, an actual practice of mindfulness as well as a starting point, a foundation, for even greater mindfulness. You can, if you want, write down your observations in notebooks — although there is a real danger that will turn into just more intellectualization — but the important thing is to get clear, accurate pictures in your mind. So you get a clearer and clearer collection of understandings about what you *actually* do and feel, your patterns of behavior and inner reactions, etc.

Again I want to stress that the important thing here is that self-observation is not merely intellectual analysis. This is not sitting down at nine o'clock in the evening thinking, "I was a little tense at the grocery store checkout today. Let me try to figure out what that was about. If I mix a little Freud, a little Adler and a little sociodynamics group theory here, I can come up with a plausible theory of why I felt that way and why I said what I said." It's not that. There are some places for theory in mindfulness practice, but the essence of it is that you learn at the time you're at the store, in the checkout line, feeling a little tense, learn by enhanced observation *exactly* how you feel tense in that moment. Exactly how are you moving your body in that moment? Exactly what are you saying in that moment? Exactly what is the tone you're projecting in your voice when you say something in that moment? It's trying to get there on the spot, in the moment, in the here-and-now, to observe more precisely.

That trying to be there on the spot, to be more fully alive in the present moment to your experience, is what is considered, in many ways, one of the essences, if not *the* essence, of reaching some kind of enlightenment in various spiritual traditions.

I can't stress often enough that there is a widespread understanding in many spiritual traditions of this idea of living in illusion. Particularly that *we do not live in the here and now. We live in the there and then.* We live in the yesterdays and the tomorrows. We live in abstractions and, as a result, are not all that well tuned in to what is actually going on.

Now don't take that to extremes: we're all well tuned in enough that we didn't get run over by a car when we walked across the street on the way here today. We've got the minimum contact necessary for surviving in basic physical reality down (usually). Beyond that minimum there are so many more subtle things, especially in terms of our interactions with other people, whereby being even a little tuned out, you miss or distort your perception of important things. So you act in ways that are maladaptive, not quite tuned in, and you reap the consequences of your (mis)perceptions and actions.

So we come to the act of committing yourself to self-observe, to self-remember. What are you doing, perceiving, feeling *at this moment*? What *exactly* are you doing at this moment? As this attitude of open minded, essentially scientific curiosity becomes a prominent part of your mental patterns, it begins to make a shift toward living in reality, toward living in the moment. In the long run, this changes your life.

It's not that you're deliberately trying to change anything, but it happens. For example, you may have the experience of saying something to a friend and, an hour later, you realize it was quite inadvertently insulting to the person you said it to and, unfortunately, it's too late to say anything to change it now. Later she talked about your insulting behavior to mutual friends, etc. We all, unfortunately, know how these things go from too much direct experience! But suppose that within a minute after you said something stupid, before she walked off, you were present enough to realize what you'd done? You would have a chance to tell your friend "Ah! Wait, excuse me I just said something really stupid!" Suppose you were present enough that, as you started to open your mouth and say it, you realized right then and there, "I'm really about to say something stupid. I'm going to be sorry!" and stopped yourself. If you learn to live in the present, there is a chance to do this.

There is a nice analogy I might share with you from an important book by Robert DeRopp. The name of the book is *The Master Game* (de Ropp 1968). He talked about our minds as being like a city — a walled, medieval city — and like any city, there are a lot of different neighborhoods. There are parts of the mind city where there are libraries and art museums, parts where there are police stations and jails, nice residential areas, and parts that are slums with very slimy characters living in them and whatnot. The mind city, unfortunately, has a rather ineffective central government which is not in very good control! In DeRopp's analogy, there are walls around the city and a lockable entrance gate, with a watchman. If the watchman was alert, he could decide who to let in and out of the city. "This one looks like an agitator who is going to go down to the slums and start a riot. I'll close the gate and not let him come in." "That one just got out of jail and is going to the next town to steal something and ruin our reputation, I won't let her out!" If you can get a fair amount of awareness into the present moment, you can exert a fair amount of control over your subsequent reactions, but once the reactions happen, they're much harder to control, and often it's too late.

I'll give you an example of this, what can happen when I'm remembering to observe myself, to keep some attention in the present moment. But I too often forget to practice this, no matter how much I value it.

Sometimes something will startle me — boom! — a loud noise happens somewhere, or something like that. My body starts to jump. Now if I'm not self-observing, self-remembering, focusing some attention to try to live close to the present, I'm going to jump, I'm going to startle — this is a hardwired physiological reaction to a sudden stimulus — and within approximately half a second to one second, the physiological reaction will have adrenaline start coursing through my body. (I say adrenaline for simplicity, given all the latest research it may actually be a mix of fifty or more informational chemicals!) The adrenaline will amplify all of my previous physiological and psychological startle reactions and I've got at least a half hour of being wired and nervous and twitchy coming! If I'm present, if I'm paying conscious attention to the here-and-now when the boom happens, though, there is still an initial jump — the sound is startling — but I instantly, mindfully, know it was just a sound and nothing else. My observation is that the adrenaline doesn't start flowing and I don't have to deal with half an hour of twitchiness consequent on this. That's just one of the simple advantages of living closer to the present. Simply committing yourself to some kind of self-observation, scientifically speaking, to try to observe the data of your life better rather than automatically getting carried away in your theories, and getting in the habit of doing it regularly, is one way to produce important changes in your life.

There are more systematic ways to change your life and

live more in the present that involves self-observation and a certain deliberate cultivation of attention. Figure 1 helps explain this.

CONSENSUS CONSCIOUSNESS:
Capturing of attention by external phenomena/stimulation.

CONSENSUS CONSCIOUSNESS:
Reactive capture of attention, following stimulation, by internal processes

SELF-REMEMBERING:
Deliberate deployment of attention

Here is the mind, represented on the left in all three phases of the diagram. Here is the external world, on the right. When something happens, you're stimulated and your attention goes out. For example, you hear a loud bang, or somebody says hello, or the phone rings. In ordinary consciousness the bulk of your attention goes out, indicated by the thick

MIND SCIENCE · 117

arrow. This is "normal," it's semi-voluntary in terms of control, it's semi-automatic attention.

Then, as the middle part of the diagram shows, our automatic habits are such that almost all of our attention might well be grabbed up by internal reactions to the external stimulus. Somebody says hello, you automatically say hello. You don't have to think about it. A loud bang and you're all wound up in fear and wondering, "Are they shooting at me?" And so forth. An apperceptive mass of mental, emotional and bodily habits is aroused by the stimulus and pretty much all your attention and energy is used up by these reactions in "normal" consciousness.

But a third style is possible, shown in the bottom third of Figure 1. Gurdjieff's primary technique for being more present, for self-remembering, is to deliberately split the arrow of attention, so that no matter what happens, you never allow all your attention to be taken by anything, be it external stimulus or internal reaction. A small amount of it is always kept in the role of observer. A small amount always goes to the "laboratory," where the inner scientist is, as it were, taking notes on what is happening specifically, this instant, then this next instant, and then this next instant, *ad infinitum*.

This deliberate split of attention can make major changes in the way you live your life. Instead of events grabbing all of your energy and then starting all the automatic psychological machinery — you know, whenever somebody looks at me that way I get such and such a kind of reaction — instead of that kind of thing mechanically and automatically happening, a new quality of experience results, which I like to term *spaciousness*. Instead of life being quite so pressed, with one reaction and action and reaction and action, etcetera, etcetera, one right after another, there is a little bit of space experienced around events. You have more time to understand them in a relaxed, holistic way, and have moments to consider what you're doing or starting to do.

I've begun describing this effect as spaciousness only lately; I wouldn't have been able to do that even a few years ago. Years ago I took several courses on meditation from a Tibetan lama, Tarthang Tulku, at the Nyingma Institute in Berkeley. One of the things he talked about in many lectures that really intrigued me was "finding the space between thoughts." I found that a fascinating concept and I thought about it a great deal but I never found any space between my thoughts! It was a great hypothesis, this space between thoughts, but my thoughts were "Zoom-zoom-zoom-zoom!" — continuous. Now I finally know what Tarthang Tulku was talking about.

The self-remembering process, the splitting of the arrow of attention, creates a little (sometimes a lot of) space around things, so life is not so hectic. There is a little more time to consider things, to act more sensibly and methodically. There is a more alive and satisfying quality to life. Now, I've explained it to you in an abstract form with the arrow of attention metaphor in Figure 1. Essentially, you always keep a little bit of your voluntarily controllable attention fueling the observing part of your mind, instead of letting all of it being attracted to anything.

For those of you who worry that not giving full attention to the outside might make you seem "inauthentic," especially if you're not giving your full attention to someone who is talking to you — I've known people to have this theoretical worry — it doesn't work that way. This may seem paradoxical on an intellectual level, but at the data level, experientially, self-remembering makes you a better person in relationships because you've become someone who actually pays attention to the other person instead of being "hypnotized" by your concepts, your theories and beliefs and reactions about them.

But enough of these introductory remarks. Let me get into the practicalities of self-remembering, of mindfulness in everyday life.

The practical way of doing this is rather like vipassana

again, or somewhat like the concentrative meditation practice, but it's adapted to everyday life. You don't have to be sitting on a special cushion in a quiet room to be able to self-observe and self-remember. The practical way is to split your attention so that a small, but significant part of your mind — it doesn't matter exactly how much — 5 percent, 10 percent, 15 percent, it varies from moment to moment — keeps track of some specified aspect of sensation in your physical body, while the rest goes about its job of *actively* looking at and generally *actively* sensing, the world around you.

The way self-remembering is usually taught is that you learn to sense your arms and legs, to keep track of the flow of sensations in your arms and legs, while simultaneously *looking* at the world around you, *listening* to the world around you (tasting it when it's appropriate, touching it when it's appropriate and so forth), always with a little attention actively paid to sensations in your arms and legs. The consequence of this practice is that instead of events and reactions coming along and automatically grabbing all your attention and activating all your habitual mental and emotional machinery, the deliberate attention to your body anchors you in the moment. Your arms and legs are never there and then: your arms and legs are always here, always now.

This deliberate focusing of attention in two directions in self-remembering has some interesting effects. First, it keeps all that automatic machinery of your mind from always going full tilt by not letting it grab all your attention. Second, even though you're paying less (automatic) attention to external things, in that they and your automated reactions to them don't automatically grab your attention, somehow you see/sense them better, more clearly and accurately than normally, because your preconceptions, your beliefs, your internal reactions don't keep clouding the picture as much as they used to. So by taking some of your attention away from your automatic reactions, you actually become better at seeing the outside world — and the outside world also becomes a much neater place! We'll wait on discussing that aspect further until we have some direct experience.

In a moment I'll show you how to do this. I want to remind you again, though, of the "ridiculousness" of what we're doing here today. To teach all of the essentials of mindfulness practice in a one day workshop? In a single book? I'm giving you a lot of rich food, but you can't digest it all. So keep trying to follow what we're doing, but don't be too hard on yourself if it doesn't all make sense and produce great results right away! It will be quite good enough if you have some tastes of what's possible on a first try, so you can see if you want to follow this up.

CHAPTER 8

Practice:
Self-Remembering

ere's how self-remembering is done. You start by doing
a meditative exercise, a body scan. It is a more directed
form of vipassana than we've done earlier today. This
body scan is an exercise that's traditionally done first thing in
the morning. You should take five to ten minutes to do it,
sometimes more if you like. Spend the time tuning into your
body sensations, particularly your arms and legs. This sensi-
tizes you to their existence and sensory qualities. It embodies
you. Then you try to keep track of arm and leg sensations
throughout the entire day, while you otherwise go about
actively perceiving your world — and all sorts of interesting
things happen when you do that.

I will guide you through the body scan, the morning exercise as it's called. Some of my students have also called this
sensitizing of the arms and legs the *priming exercise.*

You don't have to do this priming exercise before self-
re-membering, before practicing sensing, looking, and listening

throughout the day: you can just begin directly splitting attention between monitoring the body through arms and legs and perceiving the rest of the world in an active fashion. But it usually helps a lot to take a little time to sensitize yourself to it first thing in the morning.

Time constraints are such that we will have to go through this more quickly than I would like, but more details on this can be found in my books *Living the Mindful Life* (Tart 1994) or *Waking Up* (Tart 1986).

(The initial form of this exercise, as given here, should be spread over ten to twenty minutes)

Sit like we were going to do a meditation . . . Close your eyes . . . Take a minute to just settle down . . . and be comfortable . . . I'll actually give you a long form of this morning exercise which will be like an internal massage of your body . . . Even though this is a scientific conference, be prepared for a little pleasure!

Okay, now focus your attention in the way we learned this morning, with opening up meditation, on your right foot . . . and just open your mind to feeling whatever sensations there are, in your right foot, at this moment . . . Just like the vipassana meditation, there are no "good" or "bad" sensations . . . There is nothing you *should* or *shouldn't* feel . . . But just tune in to whatever you *do* feel . . .

It might be warm . . . it might be cold . . . it might itch . . . it might be numb . . . it might be warm, who knows? I don't know what your foot feels like. But you can pay attention . . .

Remember our analogy, you pay attention as if someone's giving you something delicious, some subtle creation of gourmet cooking, to taste . . . Just what is the quality of sensation in your right foot *right now*? . . .

It may be a steady sensation . . . or it might change from moment to moment . . . but just follow that quality of that sensation . . . If it feels numb, feel *exactly* what numbness feels like, moment to moment . . . If it feels like "nothing," what is the exact quality of that nothing, moment by moment?

Now shift your focus up through the ankle and into the lower part of your right leg, your calf . . . so you're now sensing the lower leg from the ankle up through the knee . . . Feel whatever the quality of sensation is there . . .

Now again remember, there is nothing you're supposed to feel or not feel . . . Just feel whatever is there . . .

Now shift your focus up to the upper half of your right leg, your thigh, from the knee through the hip . . . What's the quality of sensation there?

Just as in meditation, if your mind wanders off to other things, when you realize it's done that, just gently bring it back. . .

Now shift your focus to your right hand and sense whatever sensations there are in your right hand . . . from the fingers through the wrist . . .

Now again shift your focus, upward, to your right forearm . . . Please sense your right forearm, from the wrist through the right elbow . . . Again, I don't know what it will be like for you . . . It could be many things . . . It could be changing things . . . Whatever it is *at this instant*, just open your mind to it . . . and appreciate it in a relaxed way . . .

Now shift your attention up to the upper half of your right arm, from the elbow all the way up to and including the shoulder . . . Sense what's there . . .

Now move across your body, to the upper half of your left arm, from the shoulder down through the left elbow . . . and sense what's there . . .

Now shift your attention to your left forearm, from the elbow through the wrist . . . and sense that . . .

Now sense your left hand, from the wrist down through the fingertips . . .

Now shift your attention down to the upper half of your

left leg, from the hips down through the knee . . . sensing whatever's there . . .

Remember there is no way it's supposed to feel, just follow, open-mindedly, whatever's there . . . Moment-by-moment . . .

Now shift your focus downward to the lower half of your left leg, from the knee through the ankle . . .

And now sense your left foot . . .

Now we're going to widen our focus . . . Broaden your attention, so you sense whatever sensations or patterns of sensations there are in both feet at once . . . Whatever sensation or pattern of sensations is in both feet now, be aware of it . . . Sense its steadiness or variation from moment to moment . . .

Now widen the focus even more, so while you continue to sense both feet, you also sense both lower legs . . .

You usually have to let details of sensation go as you widen the focus, that's okay, but sense the overall pattern as well as occasional details . . .

Now broaden your focus further, and bring in all of your legs and feet . . .

Now broaden the focus even further, so in addition to sensing your feet and legs, you add in both hands . . .

And adding your forearms also . . .

And adding your upper arms as well, so now you're sensing the *whole pattern* of sensation in your arms and legs, feet and hands . . .

Now while you continue to sense the pattern of sensation in your arms and legs — and you'll automatically include hands and feet whenever I mention arms and legs — further widen the focus, so you listen to whatever sounds there are . . . So you hear the distant voices from outside the room when they are there, for instance . . . you hear my voice . . . you may hear people coughing or moving . . . and whatever other sounds occur . . .

Whatever you hear, you also simultaneously have your

attention split, so you sense sensations in your arms and legs . . .

Your hearing may include also the apparent absence of sounds, but sense the quality of auditory space around you . . .

Now broaden your focus even further, so in the next few seconds, you gently open your eyes and begin to look around the room . . . while simultaneously listening to the quality of whatever sounds there are . . . and feeling the pattern of sensations in your arms and legs . . .

Go ahead and open your eyes now, and look actively at various things in the room . . . Look at something for a few seconds . . . and then look at something else for a few seconds . . . and then look at something else for a few seconds . . . while continuing to sense your arms and legs . . . and to hear whatever sounds there are.

This looking part now is very different from the earlier meditation practices. You don't fix your eyes on anything for more than a few seconds . . . You don't park your eyes anywhere, but you *actively* look . . . Look at everything as if you've never seen it before . . . while listening, while sensing your arms and legs.

Now the way you divide your attention will vary from moment to moment . . . At times vision will take up a lot of your attention, because vision is a very dominant sense. Hearing is fairly dominant also, but try to always keep around ten percent of your attention in sensing your arms and legs . . .

As I said, look around . . . The social rule of politeness that says you must look steadily at the speaker is now rescinded! Look at other things, don't fixate on me . . .

Now how many of you feel some kind of change in the quality of your consciousness? Let me see some hands. (*Most hands go up.*) Good!

Keep up this *sensing, looking, and listening* procedure. Try to keep it up the rest of our time together. In fact, I recommend that you keep it up for the rest of your life!

What's happening is that, in a general sense, you're being more conscious, more awake, than you usually are. Instead of automatic habits and stimuli running the machinery of your mind, you're deliberately controlling what runs by the way you deploy your attention.

Could we get a few phenomenological descriptions of what people are experiencing?

STUDENT: *It was fun!*

Excellent! But I notice you spoke in the past tense. It *was* fun? Have you stopped? I'd like you to start again, you don't have to stop, okay?

STUDENT: *This is almost like a hypnotic trance induction.*

That's an interesting comparison. But there is a difference. This is a *de*-hypnosis induction!

STUDENT: *I have a keen sense of being here, now, within my body.*

Yes! That often happens. Good!

Coming back to the observation that this seems like a hypnotic induction: Because I'm speaking quietly doesn't mean it's hypnosis. I'm just slowed down because I am *here, now,* instead of drunk on my thoughts, my so-called normal state.

STUDENT: *I found I was quickly overwhelmed by it and had trouble keeping up. It was like this was some fairly advanced exercise compared to what we've done this morning, and I just actually couldn't retain that same process.*

Can you maintain it now, while you're talking with me?

STUDENT: *No.*

Can you try? Maybe with a reduced focus, such as just staying aware of just your hands while listening and looking, rather than all your arms, legs, feet and hands?

Come. I invite you to come to the present.

STUDENT: *Yes, I can do this fairly well now.*

This is advice for anyone who's having trouble keeping the wide focus. If you can't get all of your arms and legs in there, be aware of just your two hands, and the sound of my voice, and of what you're looking at.

Here's another practical suggestion. Don't stare at me fixedly, even if you're looking my way, even if I'm talking to you. Look at my nose for a few seconds, and then my shoulders, or something like that. Keep your visual attention moving around. (*Focusing back on student who was having trouble*) Is that better?

STUDENT: *Yes.*

Okay, and it's a lot simpler too.

STUDENT: *Yes, it's simpler.*

Good! You folks are reacting very well. I can get a feel for your internal condition just by the way you all are looking and acting. This is very different from the intellectual high we'll be on the rest of the week, as we hear paper after paper at this wonderful, but oh so intellectual conference!

STUDENT: *I did notice a hypnagogic pattern, I would think of one part of the instructions, then go to sleep, and then have a hypnagogic flip to another part of the instructions.*

Yes, you can get hypnagogic flips between the different parts of the instructions. It means you're sleepy.

STUDENT: *No, not really. I didn't go all the way.*

Yes, well it might not be exactly the same as ordinary sleep.

This warm up procedure, this morning exercise, this prelude to sensing, looking, and listening, does require skills similar to those required in meditation. We have to develop an ability to hold a sustained attentional focus under conditions that are difficult in some ways. We are sitting still, we're comfortable, we're not having to act. That makes it easier to slip off into sleep: but we have to maintain focus to get beyond that.

What else are people experiencing?

STUDENT: *First thing, I allowed my mind to go out, but it comes back, and while it comes back . . .*

(*Another student gets up in front row to reach for water pitcher on CTT's table while first student is still talking.*)

Excuse me, but while you're up, would you mind refilling my cup of water?

(Student slowly and mindfully refills CTT's cup)

I just got a conscious cup of water! Very good!

Please go on.

STUDENT: *My mind's still out, but it comes back, and as it comes back it's losing what's out there. I find I can't focus on both my arms and legs simultaneously, there is a momentary flip back and forth.*

Flip back and forth?

STUDENT: *Yes.*

This practice of sensing, looking, and listening is requiring a lot; you must maintain your focus on all three aspects — sensing your arms and legs, listening, looking — simultaneously. So a lot of people find they do tend to alternate back and forth, noticing, say, sounds, then sensations in the arms and legs, then what they're looking at, etc. That's good too, because if you're alternating among the three foci you're still giving *conscious direction* to your attention, which is quite different from most of what usually happens to our attention. And as I said to the gentleman in the back row there too, if it's difficult to maintain the entire arms and legs focus, you could bring it down, say, to just your hands. If that's tough you can bring it down to one hand to keep track of. Do bring in the listening and the looking along with some body part focus though, this is a practice for mindfulness in life and in almost all life situations we have to see and hear what's around us! This is not a "tripping out" meditation.

STUDENT: *I felt a sense of peace.*

I hear the past tense again. Felt? Is the sense of peace gone already?

STUDENT: *Well no, there are other things happening, even better than peace.*

Oh! Better than peace, Okay! Tell us more, that's very interesting.

STUDENT: *Since it was so peaceful, I decided I'd play with the peace, and I kind of imagined this grouping up there. Something that would normally scare me. If I focused the way I usually do, I felt frightened. If I imagined it up there and focused on my hands at the same time I could feel the fear level going away. I felt like I had a tool that I could use to deal with fear.*

Yes, you do. If you practice just sensing, looking, and listening, so it becomes a fairly readily available skill, all sorts of stressful situations will become a lot easier to handle, and there will be a great increase in clarity.

Let me give you a little conceptual help here. Now I have to watch myself closely in doing this — I'm going to talk about science for a minute, and that's a very heady drink for me, continuing with our analogy of a thoughtaholic being like an alcoholic, so I've got to discipline myself to keep some of me here, now in my body.

If you develop this sense of self remembering by sensing, looking, and listening, keeping part of yourself present by anchoring some attention in your body, I think you'll become a better scientist, because you'll stay in clearer contact with the data that you're working with. Your theorizing will be more data based, and so more likely to be accurate and useful, instead of your mind going off into flights of fancy that have so little to do with the data that someday you discover you have an apparently brilliant intellectual edifice that doesn't relate to anything in the real world.

But that's interesting to play with fear the way you did. Do any of you know about this eye movement desensitization therapy that's become so popular in the past few years? (Shapiro 1995) I don't know that much about it, but one of the things I've learned makes me suspect it's a little bit like this. They keep people moving their eyes around, and so the clients' fears can't build up to the same overwhelming level they usually do. We're moving our eyes around in a similar way, as well as paying deliberate attention to what we're looking at, and the constantly changing stimulation helps keep our attention from getting "stuck" in its habitual places, from getting completely sucked up by an emotional trap.

Another relevant concept here I learned from Carl Jung's writings, but it's of much wider relevance than the way Jung usually applied it. Jung talked about the *constellating power* of the unconscious mind. How many of you can see the constellation of the Big Dipper when you look at the sky at night?

(Almost all hands go up.)

Okay. If it's not cloudy tonight, I want you to go outside and look at it — and then try to see it for what it really is, just a bunch of random points of light. That's your homework assignment.

I don't like to bias you when I ask you to make an observation, but since we won't be meeting tomorrow I'll talk about the likely result. It's going to be real hard to do. Once we've got the idea of a constellation into our head, it controls the way our perception is constructed, and it's very hard to get away from that construction. Jung talked about powerful contents coming up from the collective unconscious, archetypes, that then constelled the rest of mental functioning around that core, but constellation is really a far more general principal about the organization of perception.

Once we have an idea, a concept of something, that concept tends to strongly bias the construction of our perceptions so we see the construct. When something fearful comes along, for example, it tends to constellate fear. It organizes, constellates everything around itself to reinforce fearful qualities, and of course the fear is then much worse. Most or all of our attention is sucked up into a highly charged construction that may seriously distort our understanding of the actual state of the world.

By having deliberately kept some attention back, through sensing, looking, and listening, through self-remembering, though, all that automatic constellation often doesn't take place. Perceptions tend to keep the intensities and qualities they actually have, rather than being grossly inflated by automatized, reactive processes. It's the same thing I talked about this morning with Shinzen Young's equation that suffering equals pain multiplied by resistance. Resistance allows automatic processes to activate, constellation takes place, something big is built up out of what may be small in reality, and we (uselessly) suffer a lot. *By deliberately controlling the deployment of our attention, we have more freedom over what's going to be built up, over how we perceive reality, as well as more accurate perception.*

STUDENT: *I've worked with the eye movement desensitization therapy. It is very powerful. You're right that the eye movements do take attention away from the problems, the fears and compulsions. That's part of it, but there is a more elaborate theory to explain why it works.*

Yes. My comments are intended to be very general because I don't have any real familiarity with the technique; just some things I've read about it.

STUDENT: *Practical stuff. I certainly experienced this state, coming into it and feeling very peaceful . . .*

You can maintain it now if you want!

STUDENT: *I'm trying to, but it's complicated, listening to what you're saying and thinking about it and trying to keep track of my arms and legs and senses. It's hard!*

That's right.

STUDENT: *And I can't imagine how I'd have any success at all when doing difficult things in my life, like programming a computer or reading a technical manual. Something that requires all my intellectual concentration. How could I handle that?*

One of my students was a computer programmer, and he had exactly the same kind of problem you're talking about, it's such an intellectually demanding job. When we would have group meetings and special work meetings, where there was social support for sensing, looking, and listening, he had a reasonable degree of success at it. But then when he sat down in front of the "hypnosis machine," as he called it — his computer at work — and all that wonderful information popped up on the screen, he was routinely lost in it. I have the same problem when I sit in front of my computer to write, get my email, etc. That sort of intellectually demanding situation is one of the most exceptionally difficult circumstances to remember yourself in.

Back in the immediate here-and-now, I notice some of you are looking at me too steadily. Remember not to stare fixedly when you're sensing, looking, and listening, look *consciously*, *deliberately* at something for a few seconds and then deliberately switch to something else.

If you take an absolutist view, if you believe that if you're not doing this sensing, looking, and listening just right then you're not doing anything worthwhile, then you set yourself up for lots of failure experiences. There are times when it's adaptive and appropriate to be highly absorbed in particular kinds of tasks, like writing a computer program, especially if it's a safe environment that is unlikely to make unexpected demands on you. When a task stretches the limits of your capacity and skill, you really have to give it a hundred percent of your attention. But, do you ever get a drink of water? Ever go to the bathroom? Ever take a lunch break? It's practical in a situation like that to make use of the break times to come back out of the trance, as it were, of being totally absorbed in the task, to then be present in each action of the break. As you walk to the water cooler, be aware of how each step you take feels, the action of filling your cup, what drinking the water actually feels like moment-to-moment, etc. And then you do go home from the job occasionally, right? Do you want to mentally take your job home with you and live in the abstractions and thoughts about it forever, or would you like some breaks for living in reality, in sensuality, in the here-and-now?

I want to address this concern realistically, not just apply perfectionistic standards that might be appropriate for monks and nuns but not for the rest of us. I'm giving you a taste of a possible way of living that's quite wonderful and useful, but I'll be the first to admit that it's very hard to do it and sustain it. *Our social system has no use for awake people*, so there is no social reinforcement and reward for becoming more awake. People who run as mechanical robots can do perfectly fine within our social system — ignoring the bigger picture. There is a niche for every one of them, even if it's in a negative role; mindlessness increases social stability, in a strange sense. This is one of the terrible senses of Gurdjieff's statement that you don't need psychology to understand people, you need mechanics.

Sometimes when people ask me what kind of psychologist I am, I tell them I'm a "transpersonal behaviorist." I think we have extraordinary spiritual *potentials*, but most of the time the behaviorists were right; there is no need to postulate a mind and we can be understood as habit driven, conditioned biological machines. And that mechanical life can be our total fate. But, even if we don't have a usual social situation that promotes coming to our senses — and there is that wonderful old folk phrase, "coming to your senses" that has so much wisdom in it — right *now* you are coming to your senses! Anybody notice that in addition to hearing and looking, other senses are sharper? Anybody notice that things are brighter than they were, for instance?

STUDENT: *Yes, this rug. It's really quite striking and interesting!*

Ah, yes, yes! And before we did this it was just a "hotel carpet," just dull, uninteresting, largely unperceived background.

If you learn to come to your senses this way, when you practice sensing, looking, and listening, you will discover a very interesting secret. *We live in an art museum!* Everywhere you go, you'll find striking, vital, often beautiful and *alive* things and people in the world, even in conventionally negative circumstances, instead of that same old world you've lost interest in and pay little attention to. Sensing, looking and listening freshens the world instead of letting us get lost in that dulling "Been, there, done that!" attitude.

Let's take am attention practice break. I don't want to overly tire your "voluntary attention muscles." I'll get real intellectual for a minute and let you relax. Space out for a second, while I tell you this one.

One of Gurdjieff's most interesting ideas was about what he called the *food of impressions*. He taught that, quite aside from the specific information particular sensory stimuli give us, they also act as a kind of food, a kind of nourishment for our nervous system, and our nervous system needs that nourishment. We recognize the need for a balanced and adequate diet on a physiological level. We can get deficiency diseases. If we don't get enough vitamin C, for example, we get scurvy. There are all sorts of stresses we're more vulnerable to if we don't have proper nourishment or proper diet. Gurdjieff said the same thing holds true psychologically: if we don't get the proper food of impressions, we suffer from psychological deficiency diseases.

One of these deficiency diseases resulting from a lack of balanced and quality sensory impressions manifests itself as some (un- or semi-conscious) part of us knowing that we're not really alive, that we're not really healthy, so as a consequence we're desperately looking for more stimulation, anything to try to fill the lack. So we get addicted to gross, crass, emotionally intense stimulation. The television is on 18 hours a day showing us violence and disaster, we drive recklessly ("I fear, therefore I am," to grossly modify Descartes' "Cogito, ergo sum."), we read in the papers about all the murders, wars, and disasters, we unconsciously create trouble with our loved ones ("I'm feeling strong emotions in this argument, therefore I am"), etcetera — we're trying to get enough nutrition from impressions by eating mental junk food, trying to fill our need with *quantity* when we don't know how to get *quality*. It's better than nothing, than sensory starvation, but it doesn't nourish well, for in our pursuit of quantity the quality of the food of impressions is poor (vitamin deficiencies) and contains all sorts of toxins.

From Gurdjieff's point of view, for instance, we'll always have wars because all that terrible excitement gives us a large quantity of impression nourishment, it shocks us into a little bit more wakefulness. I recall that Studs Terkel wrote a book about people's memories of the second World War (Terkel 1984), for instance, and most people remembered the war as the most alive and vital time in their lives! The costs, both in the real world and in our psyches, are terrible, of course.

But if you come to your senses, practice this kind of self-remembering — and *we're coming back to our senses now*, our space-out break is over — then ordinary events give us far more nourishment of this food of impressions, because we're *present* for them. Both the quantity and the quality go up, and the toxins of negative inner reactions are reduced. You don't need to have a fifty-thousand-dollar painting hanging on your wall to appreciate visual beauty! Just about anything you look at, *if* you're present there, practicing this self-remembering process, is more vivid, more alive, more beautiful! It's really quite incredible. It nourishes you in a very real sense.

I don't know how to completely translate the idea of food of impressions into conventional psychological terms yet, and I don't think we have the psychological research to back it up, but I think Gurdjieff was definitely on to something. It makes sense to me, personally, from my direct experience.

STUDENT: *This is producing a very nice experience, but it's going against habit to deliberately use attention like this, and it takes energy. I'm working at it! But I'm worried that the force of habit will take over and perhaps it will spoil the experience?*

That's good thinking, to be concerned with preventing the habituation of the experience of sensing, looking, and listening. One of our greatest strengths and our greatest curses is we can habituate anything. *We can automatize any psychological functioning in life*, and it's quite clear to me that you can literally go through life without any "real," non-automatized consciousness. The possibilities of consciousness can be automatically "used up" in the "machinery" of the ordinary self, with life being mainly a reaction rather than a conscious, free action.

Earlier somebody brought up what philosopher David Chalmers has termed the hard problem of consciousness (Chalmers 1996), how consciousness, whose nature seems so obviously different from physical matter, can arise from a physical brain. For part of a technical answer, you could see the little commentary I wrote for the zombie issue of the *Journal of Consciousness Studies* (Tart 1995). But I tend to agree with Gurdjieff in many ways that ordinarily there is no "consciousness" around to worry about. There is a stream of experience, but it's largely a passive, reactive stream of experience. Things happen to us, the machinery takes over, experiences and reactions happen. There are very few of the properties we habitually attribute to consciousness, such as free will, discrimination, and so forth. Everything happens on a more mechanical level. *But there can be real consciousness.*

Now habituation is indeed the enemy. *Deliberate*, conscious variety in mental functioning is an important way of fighting habituation. So, in addition to this general practice of bringing attention to the present by dividing it among sensing, looking, and listening, Gurdjieff taught many special exercises to cultivate conscious attention and will even more intensely. For example, always notice, when you walk through a doorway, which foot goes through first.

Now that sounds like a silly thing to waste your effort on, except that the act of walking through doorways is something that you do many times a day without really being conscious of the act. By training yourself to become deliberately aware of this action, you can become more generally conscious, for aside from the specifics, you are training will and intention in general.

But this kind of exercise can become automatized too. I remember visiting the Green Gulch Zen Center north of San Francisco once, and they told visitors they had a mindfulness rule there that you always went through doors with your left foot first. I thought that was neat and very Zen, I wouldn't argue against doing that — as a temporary practice. But from what I've understood from Gurdjieff and modern psychology and my own experience, I think going through doors with your left foot first will work well to make you more conscious for a while. And then, all too soon, you'll simply have the automatic habit of stepping through doors with your left foot first, perhaps accompanied by the automatic thought of "I am being mindful."

That's the worst part of it, see? You can *think about* this sensing, looking, and listening without actually *doing* it. You can think about being more present without actually doing it. *The only real answer to the habituation and automatization problem is a frequently reaffirmed commitment to really wanting to be present, and a constant examination of your own mind and experience.* You need to directly see when you have indeed substituted the thought of the practice for the actual practice.

One of the disciplines that I try to practice, for instance, is that when I get up and talk to people and do a workshop like this about being more present, I have to be really careful and observe myself so as not talk about the qualities of being present when I'm not being present. It happens sometimes — I blather on about being present, paying attention to the here-and-now, when I'm hypnotized by my thoughts and way out of touch.

We can automatize anything, and it's terrible. You can "live" your whole life in automatized abstractions and not even know it. So in response to your concern about habituation taking over your practice, yes, it's a big problem. You can set up specific exercises and keep changing them constantly as an important way of dealing with that. Deliberate novelty helps. You can do some specific practice, like observing which foot you enter a doorway with, or always entering with a specified foot, but keep checking, and if it "wears out" after a week, if you're comfortably and automatically slipping into thoughts about the practice instead of actually doing it, change to a new one. If it lasts for two weeks, good.

STUDENT: *What happens if you no longer habituate any experience?*

I don't know if total dishabituation, deautomatization, is possible. There are so many automatisms in our body and mind! But what could change in a very large way is that instead of 99.999 percent of your responses being automatized, maybe they could go down to 95 percent or 90 percent. If that happens, there will be a major change in the way in which you experience life.

Also, if you make lots of these efforts to be more present, even if you can't manage to feel that you are strongly mindful, attentive at all moments, after a lot of practice there does become a change. The change is that potential mindfulness is not as "far away." When you want to bring your attention to the here-and-now, to better observe external and internal reality, instead of fuller consciousness, mindfulness, being, by analogy, a mile below the surface in our ordinary state, it's only five hundred feet below the surface. When circumstances or intention call for it, you can get to the surface, to greater mindfulness, much easier — instead of three days later saying, "Gosh, if only I'd been more aware when I was having that fight and saying those stupid things!"

Okay, are people remembering to sense their arms and legs in spite of this rather conceptual talk?

(A fair number of hands go up)

Wait one minute on more questions; let me change the quality of our experience a little bit now.

Close your eyes one moment . . . sense your arms and legs . . . This is just a little refresher dip into your body now . . . Feel your arms and legs . . . Add hearing to your experience . . . Slowly open your eyes . . . Now for about three or four seconds each, look three or four other people in the eye, one after another, while continuing to sense your arms and legs and look and listen . . .

Okay, now with that little refresher under our belts, we can have your questions.

STUDENT: *Sometimes while I'm sensing, looking, and listening, I will remember something that the situation reminds me of, and the memories seem more vivid than usual, they feel like living memories.*

That's interesting that it's enhanced your memories, that when you do it, the memories are more vivid. That's partially true for me, although memory has never been my strong point. Sensing, looking, and listening enhances my present experience, but it usually doesn't do too much for memories one way or the other. I'm still forgetful. Fortunately as a professor I have a social license for absentmindedness that gives me an acceptable excuse for forgetting!

STUDENT: *But isn't part of that because it's so easy to get distracted and not remember? When I'm really present, I do remember more vividly. It's the times that I'm unconsciously doing things, getting on with my life, that I really lose it. So I would agree with that.*

Yes, I think most people's experience is that memory for things done while more present is indeed more solid than memory of events occurring in our ordinary, samsaric sleep state.

STUDENT: *I'm wondering, Dr. Tart, why is the torso left out in the morning exercise and in later sensing, looking, and listening?*

I have three reasons for not deliberately directing your attention to your torso. First, that's the way I learned it from people teaching it as Gurdjieff presumably taught it. Second, simply adding in torso sensations creates a lot more stimulation to keep track of, and that makes it harder for many people. But the reason I give most theoretical importance to is that, based on some psychotherapeutic research, there is evidence that some of our emotional traumas are literally "stored" in the body. They correspond with or are correlated with sensations in particular body locations, and those locations are usually in the torso. Very few people have traumas "stored" in their forearms, for instance, but when you get into the belly, the heart, etc., you are in potentially active areas.

So, if you tell people to keep track of their whole body sensations, you might at some times accidentally push people into activating areas where traumatic memories are stored. That's the theoretical reasoning that's led me to stay away from focusing people on their torsos. I don't know how generally important it is, and I'm sure that while it might be an important consideration for some people, it's not for others. I teach sensing your arms and legs as your basic body reference point in the here-and-now, but if the rest of your body comes in naturally, that's fine. Personally I sense, look, and listen as a whole body exercise. But the traditional way of teaching it is with just the arms and legs.

STUDENT: *As a matter of fact we're trying to isolate the arms and legs from the rest of the body sensation. I have real difficulty with that, having worked on whole body sensation in other work.*

Yes, right. I hear a quality in your voice that suggests to me that you're not sensing, looking, and listening any more. I haven't given my usual admonition that if you ask a question, be sure to continue to sense, look, and listen while you do that. I'd like to recommend that now, although I know it is difficult to talk and stay conscious for most of us. It's a sad comment on the human race, but when we open our mouth, the clarity of our consciousness usually disappears. We're deeply "hypnotized" by the action of speaking. However I invite you to try that and, in fact, I think you'll find your questions will be more interesting if you can continue the sensing, looking, and listening process while you ask them.

STUDENT: *I'm wondering if perhaps an artist might have an easier time with this? Artists are more in touch with their environ-*

ments, especially with the visual qualities of the world.

Are you an artist?

STUDENT: *Yes, I was an artist, among other things. And I take different kinds of group work back at home all the time.*

I don't know if this would be easier for artists or not. I suspect "artists" is not a homogeneous category. There are probably many different kinds of people lumped together under that label. The ability to notice things in the external world more precisely could come about because you're doing something like this sensing, looking, and listening, or it could simply be training that's become mechanical, in a sense, a habit of paying more attention to specific sensory qualities of things. So, I don't know. Or it could occur more naturally among artists.

Speaking of natural, the two opening stanzas of Wordsworth's poem *Intimations of Immortality* are apropos here:

> *There was a time when meadow grove and stream,*
> *The Earth and every common sight,*
> *To me did seem appareled in celestial light,*
> *The glory and the freshness of a dream,*

Then he has to switch to his (and our) "normal" adult perspective.

> *It is not now as I have known of yore,*
> *Turn whereso'er I may, by night or day,*
> *The light which I have seen,*
> *I now can see no more.*

In my more pedestrian prose, Wordsworth is talking about the automatization of consciousness, about Gurdjieff's depiction of "normal" consciousness as a kind of sleep or dream state. Children seem to have more natural vitality, more awareness; they live in a more interesting, more sensuous world. But we're too busy and "important" for that — and we live impoverished lives as a result.

STUDENT: *I have some comments on that. I want to run this by you. You've given us deliberate procedures for tuning in better to the world, but my experience is that this can happen naturally sometimes, when you're in an especially good mood. Isn't it somewhat unnatural to split your attention this way? Are the results of natural openings and this exercise similar?*

I think you're talking about something similar, yes. Sensing, looking, and listening does not have to be a totally artificial exercise in exerting ourselves, as a deliberate act of will. Certain natural circumstances can make it easier for us to split our attention that way, rather spontaneously, and certain ones can make it harder. Modern life generally makes it harder.

For instance, when the Hindus and Buddhists of earlier times talked about living in maya or samsara, I think what they didn't fully anticipate is that we now have the most technologically "advanced" samsara that's ever existed on the face of the planet! You need never have a moment alone with your own mind in our culture now! You will soon (already for some) be able to get hundreds of channels of satellite television and radio shows, you can receive enormous amounts of junk mail and magazines, you can spend all your waking hours in chat rooms on the net, or following the news! In our materially rich West, many of us can distract ourselves much of our entire lives. This includes using work as a distraction. We distract ourselves from what is essential — and much of modern life is continuous distraction. Even our idea of a "vacation" — let's go see this site, then rush to this place, and then that site, and then this site, etc., etc. — can be just another way of distracting ourselves from what is essential. Cramming in vast *quantities* of low quality "food of impressions" (the sensory impressions would be high quality *if* the places were looked at more consciously) to try to make up for the lack of *quality* in life is a desperate and high cost strategy that only partially succeeds. Last summer, for example, my wife and I camped for several days in the beauty of the Grand Tetons National Park, but were amazed when one of the rangers told us the average visitor's time in the park was one hour — the time it took to drive through on the way to Yellowstone, while saying "Look at the beautiful mountains out the left window," as they zipped through! Not too many people nowadays go off to a quiet place, like a lake or forest, and just kind of slow down and *be there*, get into that slower, natural rhythm.

This is an appropriate place to introduce the distinction Gurdjieff made between *false personality* and *essence*. Essence is what we're born with. It's not exactly the same for everybody, but it's something very basic and natural. But as we grow up, essence is suppressed and often effectively killed. Our natural, vital energy is stolen from essence and a personality is created instead. Gurdjieff, however, referred to ordinary personality as "false personality." I much prefer "false personality" to the word "ego" many spiritual people use so pejoratively, because for psychologists there is a quite positive sense of ego as reality principle also. False personality is all the things you were conditioned into thinking you are, that you invest most or of all your energy into, that you hurry up to do, to do, to do . . . to do, mistakenly thinking it's you. It results from social and parental pressures that make you deny some of your feelings and perceptions ("Good boys never think about things like that!") and over invest in others ("Daddy will be so hurt if you don't become a doctor too!").

Living your life in false personality is a terribly unbalanced state of being. One of its effects is manifested for many people as existential neurosis or mid-life crisis. A woman might be in her fifties or so, she's successful by all ordinary social terms, but suddenly she starts to realize something like "I didn't really want to be a doctor! I don't like the work I do! I'm just pleasing my parents, I've wasted my life! I'm not doing anything I really believe is worthwhile!" This kind of crisis occurs when people realize that much of what they've taken to be their own selves, that they've identified with, has not been something of their choosing, and may, in fact, be contrary to their deeper impulses, their essence. That's why Gurdjieff called it *false* personality. There wasn't much of a free and conscious choice there. We were just children, manipulated and pressured by parents and culture. But the strategies we were forced to adopt to get by, to cope, even if now outmoded and maladaptive, became identified with, became *me*, became false personality, automatically running us and using up our life energy.

So getting out in the wilderness occasionally can help. Getting anywhere that's quiet to begin with, that's got a slower rhythm than our usual frantic life can help.

Are we remembering those arms and legs while I talk so conceptually? Are we sensing, looking, and listening?

STUDENT: *What about like you see more extreme yoga positions for the body, like if you have pain, or if you have chronic pain and you're always aware of your body, would that change automatically?*

I don't follow you.

STUDENT: *If you're in a little bit of pain, will you mentally slip automatically into doing this mindfulness procedure?*

You can use pain as a reminder to do this self-remembering exercise, or you can just react to it in an automated way, or do everything you can to get rid of it right away. I don't think pain does it automatically, you won't be sensing, looking, and listening just because you're in pain.

STUDENT: *Well, purposely though, I purposely sit on an uncomfortable chair, a hard chair when I meditate.*

No, I don't think painful postures are chosen to make pain split your attention. My personal experience is you cannot habituate, cannot automatize self-remembering. There has to be this at least small act of *will* to split, to direct attention. Things can come along in ordinary consciousness and split your attention, but that's just mechanical reaction. Mechanical split is not the same thing as intentional split. If you created the intentional split you might then use some pain consciously as a reminder, as a kind of "fuel," but pain *per se* won't make you self-remember.

I wonder if we should take a break for a few minutes? I invite you to continue practicing sensing, looking, and listening during the break, I don't require it. I'll tell you an amusing, but unfortunately instructive, anecdote to send you on your way to the break.

In the early 70s, after I'd been teaching at UC Davis for a few years, a colleague (Joseph Lyons) and I wanted to teach a course in humanistic psychology. Our psychology department colleagues were very suspicious of the idea. They'd heard about humanistic psychology. People have emotions and experiences in humanistic work, they would have emotions and experiences right there in the classroom! They were not at all sure emotions and experiences had any proper place in psychology or a university classroom!

So our colleagues only allowed us to teach humanistic psychology with the provision that at the beginning of the first class of each course, we would formally announce to students that while we might occasionally do an experiential exercise that invited them to have an experience, no experience was required, and anything they did or didn't experience would not affect their grade! So I invite, but don't require, you to interact with each other during the break while trying to remember to sense, look, and listen. It will be very interesting if you do.

CHAPTER 9

Toward a Science of Consciousness

There is one further conceptual item I want to mention that's important to get across today. Then we can use the rest of our time to go into more depth on any aspect of what we already covered, or branch out a little from there.

We're here for a meeting called "Toward a Science of Consciousness." There are many different ideas of what it means to have a "science" of consciousness. For some disciplines, it means explaining consciousness *away* in a materialistic framework, to be able to say that consciousness is nothing but the activity of brain cells in nucleus number 3,217,469 or something like that. I'm glad people are doing research to elucidate the way the brain works. The brain certainly has a major and vital involvement in consciousness, but I'm mainly interested in consciousness *per se*. I don't think we should readily buy into an attitude like "Well, our interest in consciousness is something we have to tolerate until the physicists or the neurologists really explain it (away) for us, and then it will no longer be a puzzle." *I am consciousness.* My experience of my consciousness is the most direct data about reality that I have. I've got a vitally important association with my body and my nervous system too, but I am consciousness. *The quality of that consciousness is the quality of my life.*

I'm not solipsistic enough to think I'm the only one who possesses basic consciousness. I think all you folks are conscious too. We've been talking about ways in which each of us, as individuals, could become better able to observe consciousness, and, as our personal knowledge of our own consciousness increases, the freedom we have, the ability to use and control that consciousness, also increases. But let's move our thinking now to the shared social level, toward developing a science of consciousness, toward a body of socially shared knowledge, such that our individual knowledge could be expanded and enriched by consultation with that shared knowledge, by interaction with other conscious minds. I could go out and gradually figure out all the principles of chemistry myself, but I would sure get a boost by picking up a textbook on chemistry. Can we get a similar textbook on consciousness?

I mentioned earlier that, historically, psychology in the last century tried to be a science of the mind, tried to be an introspective science of consciousness — and it didn't work very well. The two big problems I mentioned were lack of trained observers and experimenter bias. The Herr Doctor Professor's theories needed to be proved if you were going to keep your job, and it probably wasn't even conscious faking: the introspective observers' own experiences were probably shaped by the biases they were consciously and unconsciously subjected to, so they manifested in that form, and sure enough, they saw what they "should" have seen. Believing is seeing, to reverse the old statement. Can we get a better science of consciousness?

I want to speculate about Buddhism for a moment as a possible science of consciousness (and as a possibly attractive activity for those of you who seriously want to further develop meditative mindfulness). Here is a tradition started by someone who, as I mentioned earlier, effectively said "Don't take anything on authority. Here are the methods for observing your mind and its nature. Go in there and figure it out for yourself!" This is not just for yourself, actually, for the more awake and enlightened you get, the less harm you do others and the more helpful you are.

Here is an inspiring translation of what the Buddha actually said, in a translation of the *Sutta to the Kalamas*, by Gates (Gates 1989):

> *Do not believe in anything simply because you have heard it.*
>
> *Do not believe in traditions because they have been handed down for many generations.*
>
> *Do not believe in anything because it is spoken and rumored by many.*
>
> *Do not believe in anything simply because it is found written in your religious books.*
>
> *Do not believe in anything merely on the authority of your teachers and elders.*
>
> *But after observation and analysis, when you find that anything agrees with reason, and is conducive to the good and benefit of one and all, then accept it and live up to it.*

STUDENT: *Before you go to say anything further, sir, I need some clarification. How do you define mind?*

I cannot define mind! I cannot define consciousness, and neither can anyone else. I must say that I find it kind of amusing that people try.

Whatever mind or consciousness is, one of its small subfunctions is defining things. The belief that somehow this small sub-function of the totality can define the totality. I mean, that's really weird! I am one, I am a consciousness, a mind. I can learn things about consciousness and mind by observing my own mind and indirectly observing those of others. Personally, I'm not too worried that I can't "define" mind or consciousness. Hopefully, I can point at the aspects or qualities of mind or consciousness that are important in particular contexts.

STUDENT: *The paradox is I know what is happening, but I cannot define it either. If I say "I study cats," I can point at a cat, I know what a cat is. There is a difference between the actual cat, which I can study, and the label "cat." But in a sense what we've been talking about today is the label!*

That's right. But in a sense, everything I've been *talking* about to this moment is trying to remind us that *the label, the name, is not the reality, but we can pay clearer attention to the reality of consciousness, and it will be greatly to our advantage to do so.* I don't know whether we can ultimately grasp "reality" in any final sense, but we can sure get closer to it.

This reminds me of a friend of mine who once told about an LSD experience she had, which was a profound, mystical experience for her. For a lot of people psychedelics can, under the right circumstances, lead to very profound experiences. In her experience, she saw the Great Truths of the Cosmos written in giant words in the sky! Well, okay, I'm sure it was a mystical experience for her, a great step forward in her understanding, but somehow I think ultimate reality may be beyond anything we can write, and words we can use. Words can be useful pointers to direct our attention, as long as we don't get carried away by them.

So I'm not too worried about any kind of ultimate definition. Reality is what is important, and will be what it is, whether we can tie it tightly in a net of words or not. But I am worried about focusing us back on sensing, looking, and listening, *now!* I'm worried that we can too easily follow our lifelong habits of getting lost in concepts and abstractions about reality instead of having much contact with it!

I see you raising your hand again. You're not going to ask me to define reality, are you?

STUDENT: *Philosopher David Chalmers suggested in a paper that we might take experience as a starting point, taking experience as primary, and it seems that you have a similar position and that it would avail us to do this.*

I do take experience as primary. Experience is certainly primary for me. I am my experience! Now when I think about my experience (which thinking activity is part of my experience, of course, a particular kind of experience), I start making classifications. One of those classifications is the so-called real, physical world. What that effectively means is that certain categories of my experience show a great consistency among themselves and a quite lawful, predictable interrelationship, such that, as a *tentative working hypothesis*, I theorize that those things exist outside me, independent of my consciousness.

The theory of an independently existing physical world, with characteristics generally independent of other aspects of my consciousness, is a very good working hypothesis, right? I don't believe that I have to make any kind of effort to insure that the molecules of the table relate to each other in such a way that the table manifests as "solid," for example, in order to hold my glass of water in place, I think they'll do their thing without my having to worry about it. This theory of an independently existing physical world is very relaxing to my mind.

But this experience of seeing the apparently independently existing glass of water sitting on the apparently independently existing table in front of me, with no effort on my part to maintain it, is still an *experience* in terms of what's directly available to me. The idea of an independently existing physical world is still just a tentative, if very useful and appealing, working hypothesis.

But many people have gone on beyond this point: they have not only hypothesized this outside world that exists independently of us, they've gotten so involved in the particulars of it that the independent reality of the physical world is no longer recognized as a working hypothesis. It has made a psychological leap into an obvious, unquestioned truth, the only and ultimate reality. Experience *per se* now becomes a mystery to explain. Indeed, many then call experience some sort of "epiphenomenon," a fancy philosophical way of making experience, consciousness, secondary and unimportant because we can't imagine a physical basis for consciousness. I've always found this line of "progress" quite amazing and amusing: we start from direct experience, we've noticed some consistent and interrelated experiences, hypothesized an independent physical world, got so enamored of it that experience no longer makes sense in this (more restricted) physical framework, and now our primary starting point, actual, direct experience has gone away? I'm not going to worry about that one!

Let's talk about a science of consciousness. Buddhism can be a very interesting example to discuss in this context. As I said earlier, the Buddha was not authoritarian. He said look, here are tools for examining your own mind, they can lead you to some very important insights about your self and the nature of reality, try them. If it works for you, great! If it doesn't work for you, certainly don't believe them. Don't believe them because the Buddha said so, that's the last thing you should do. I think that if the Buddha were alive today, he would be very unhappy at all the "Buddhists" there are, the people who believe he's some kind of divine being who gave us The Truth which we should passively accept. I make that last statement with respect to popular Buddhism, of course, not the much smaller active meditational tradition within Buddhism. It looks like there might be something within that meditation tradition that we modern Westerners would recognize as a science of mind there, or at least the beginnings of one.

What do we see in the active Buddhist meditation tradition? People are taught some basic methods for observing the mind, meditation techniques, and then spend years assiduously making observations within the "laboratories" of their own minds, using, as it were, the "microscope" of meditation to look at the finer structure of the mind. They share their observations in interpersonal contact and teaching, and in the long-lasting communications of their written scriptures. As a result of their own observations and reflections, many of them continue to make the same claim the Buddha did, namely, that this corpus of knowledge is not a belief system. Rather, it is valid and useful information about reality.

These meditation techniques (coupled with moral and practical rules for living your life, which are considered an essential part of the training) are thus repeatedly claimed to be the tools by which you also can personally verify that what they talk and write about is indeed the real nature of the mind. These advanced practitioners, our observers of mind, will explain to us what they can about their discoveries and understandings about the true nature of the mind and reality. But at the same time they will acknowledge that much of what they have learned can't really be adequately explained in words because words, logic and language, are only a small part of the totality of mind — not to mention that our ordinary consciousness, where we are so attached to words, is terribly deluded anyway. But they continue to claim that here are the procedures you can go through to understand what mind is in a profound way.

That sounds a lot like an essential science. Trained practitioners, using refined methods to make precise observations, reaching certain kinds of conclusions, communicating them to their peers. But from our Western perspective we are really curious: is it a "science," or is it a "religion"?

The working distinction I'll make, for our purposes, between a science and a religion is that a "science" really is open-minded and open-ended. A "science" takes the attitude that we don't know everything, but we want to find out, find out following the methods of essential science that I talked about earlier. What we make of what we find out, the hypotheses, the theories to explain the data, is *always* open to further test, as the data is always the primary determinant. A "religion," on the other hand, believes that basically they have got all the important truth down. It might need a little refinement in a few technical areas, but basically there are no important, fundamental questions: they have already been given the truth of everything that's important to know.

Now Buddhism — "Buddhism" is a term invented by Western missionaries, incidentally, to categorize a wide variety of beliefs and practices — clearly can become a religion, and for most people who call themselves Buddhists, it is. The Buddhist authority figures, quoting scripture which is not to be questioned, tell you the way things are, and you try to live your life in accordance with that. Most Buddhists actually don't meditate much at all. They try to live a moral life and give alms to the monks and nuns. The monks and nuns, the professionals, as it were, do the meditation practices, under the shared belief that these monks and nuns meditating helps all the people in the world, especially those generous souls who help support the monks and nuns. I'm oversimplifying terribly, of course. That's quite parallel to Western religion, where ordinary folk try to live a moral life and create merit by acts of charity and kindness, but leave the advanced stuff to the professionals.

But there are many "serious professionals" in Buddhism, even if they are a small percentage of the total population we might label Buddhist. Many of them have devoted thousands of hours to meditative and related practices. Perhaps these are the "scientists" of Buddhism? Replicating and extending basic observations and testing theories?

So, could we do something similar? Could we train people in meditative methods so they became essentially scientific, relatively objective, observers of the mind?

We would need to begin with training them in methods of

calming the ordinary mind, because, as we discussed earlier, ordinary mind is not very good for studying consciousness in our own, internal "laboratories." The ordinary mind is so agitated all the time, so busy. You can't, returning to our lake analogy, see through the surface to the deeper parts of it because of all the waves of thought and emotion on the surface. Could we train people in the concentrative methods whose prime effect is to calm that storm, so the mind begins to get transparent? Can we then train people to look through the surface, into the depth, by paying closer attention, as in the vipassana approach? And could these people then start not only to learn things about the mind, get data for themselves, but share it with other people, so that a social body of knowledge would now be built up that would enhance the understanding of all?

Now what I'm proposing as an inner-directed, introspective science is not quite the typical Buddhist model, where an individual will eventually arrive at full enlightenment, know everything there is to be known, and can only partially share knowledge with the vast majority of us who are unenlightened. But maybe we could do more. Maybe we could have a more advanced practice, a better social sharing of knowledge, which is an essential aspect of a science?

There are parallels between classical Buddhist practice and essential science, but there are important differences too. Remember when I talked about induction techniques for altered states of consciousness? I said earlier there is the formal, obvious induction technique and there is the context the technique is used in, a context with certain (explicit and implicit) expectations. When a Buddhist in a Buddhist culture is taught any of these basic meditation practices, for instance, they're not taught the practice in quite as simple a form as I've taught it today. They're taught these basic technical practices of concentrative and vipassana meditation, but both the teachers and the students bring expectations to the teaching and practice about what these meditation procedures are supposed to do; they lead them towards "enlightenment," and reduce or "purify" their bad "karma." I've put "enlightenment," "purify," and "karma" in quotes here to remind us that these are very complex, culturally laden constructs.

This teaching and meditation practice situation that we're focused on is just like any social situation. Besides the explicit cultural trappings, there are a lot of expectations that are relatively implicit but are frequently reinforced in the course of social interaction all the time. Thus a person with a Buddhist background or belief system who learns Buddhist meditation in a Buddhist context is not learning it with the same set and setting as a Western scientist.

A Western scientist, in an ideal sense, is interested in some area of reality, knows that we don't know the final answers about it, is strongly curious about it, and makes the assumption that if she or he learns the methods and techniques appropriate to that field, she or he can make a contribution, expand our knowledge of that field. That is, our culture has a model that our knowledge is definitely incomplete but can be added to through an application of scientific methods. We believe in progress.

The Buddhist model, on the other hand (as I understand it), tends to assume that all important knowledge is complete to those who have become enlightened, become Buddhas, and any individual can verify that in an empirical way by becoming a Buddha. Future Buddhas won't know more than past Buddhas, so there is no "progress" as in the typical Western model. By having that set, someone who is a good Buddhist, learning the same meditation technique, has explicit and implicit expectations influencing what will happen and how to then further proceed, compared to someone who simply says "This is a technique to explore the mind. I'm open to whatever happens. I may learn things that haven't been known before."

So the ideal scientific approach to explore what meditation can do to discover things about the mind would be to train a group of skilled practitioners who had no expectations whatsoever about what's supposed to happen as a result of practicing meditation.

Now that's a wonderful ideal, but where do you find any people who have no expectations whatsoever about what's supposed to happen? Anyone who's alive has enormous numbers of implicit and expectations about what's supposed to happen in all sorts of circumstances, and to pretend that you can somehow work with "unbiased" people who have no expectations in any areas of life is to delude yourself and undermine your research. The outcome of your research may well be mainly a function of biases and expectations you're not aware of, rather than the formal psychological factors to which you mistakenly attribute your results.

My favorite example of how powerful and misleading expectations can be comes from sensory deprivation research. For years it was "known" in the psychological and psychiatric literature that sensory deprivation was a powerful psychological (and basically physiological) technique that drove people at least partially nuts. The physiological theory explained the psychological effects of sensory deprivation by pointing out that the nervous system is dependent on the stimulation received from incoming sensory stimulation to keep various physical centers of the brain operating in the proper kind of balance. So if you put somebody in a dark, quiet room, where they didn't move at all (to eliminate tactile and proprioceptive stimulation), the resulting elimination of sensory nerve impulses was such that you literally caused a nervous system imbalance that made the brain go nuts, and so, of course, the psychological functioning of the brain was nuts. Excuse me for using a technical term like "nuts," but it conveys the essence of the technical version!

This understanding of sensory deprivation was a well-accepted conclusion in the psychological and psychiatric literature. There seemed to be a lot of experimental results to prove it. I remember reading articles that went into great detail on exactly how the physiology worked to produce the effect. It involved the reticular activating system and interacting brain centers. Sensory deprivation seemed to be a clear, well understood phenomena.

Then a man named Scheibe, working with a prominent psychiatrist, Martin Orne (Orne 1964), carried out a very interesting experiment. The actual experimental treatment was not sensory deprivation. It was two hours in a situation that would ordinarily just be thought of as boring. In the actual experimental treatment, an individual subject was put into a small room, which had no windows, but the lights were on, so it wasn't dark, and it wasn't a soundproof room. It was in a hospital, and the walls were not that thick. You could hear people's heels clicking on the floor as they walked by in the corridor outside, you could hear a little bit of the Muzak system through the walls, bits of not-quite-loud-enough-to-be-intelligible conversation of passersby, etcetera, and the subject's movement wasn't particularly restricted. The subject sat on a wooden chair at a wooden table for a couple of hours, but he wasn't lying on a soft mattress with arms and legs swathed in thick cotton pads to eliminate movement and tactile sensation, or floating in a tank of water at body temperature, as in classical sensory deprivation experiments. It was boring because there was nothing to do. There was nothing to read or anything like that. It's what most of us would consider a boring situation, but not generally what we would consider a high stress or high strangeness or "psychotomimetic" situation.

There was a "panic button" mounted on the wall. An individual subject, if he couldn't stand the procedure before the experimenter came back, could press the button.

A subject selected for the control group treatment would

arrive at the hospital lobby and Scheibe, dressed casually, would meet him, explain that he (Scheibe) was a graduate student doing his thesis, and that he had to have people sit in this room for a couple of hours and give them a questionnaire afterwards asking what their experience had been like. He took the subject into the treatment room and casually told him that if he couldn't stand it, he could press the button on the wall. Then Scheibe went away, and came back in a couple of hours.

Well, nobody in the control group pressed the button, and, as you would expect, basically the reports subjects gave on the questionnaire were that they were bored, and that was about it.

In the experimental condition, a subject would come in to the hospital lobby but Scheibe would meet him wearing a suit, a white lab coat with a stethoscope stuck in the pocket, and an official name tag, introduce himself as Dr. Scheibe, a psychiatrist. Now immediately the expectational context becomes very different from that set up for the control group subjects. If you're participating in an experiment that a psychiatrist is conducting, what do psychiatrists study?

STUDENT: *They study nuts!*

Right.

Scheibe then took the subject to an interview room where he administered a standard psychiatric intake interview, the kind that's used to decide whether somebody is psychotic enough to need to be hospitalized. During this interview there was a tray of hypodermic syringes over against the wall labeled "Emergency Tray." Scheibe didn't say anything about that tray, but it was there in plain sight. If a subject asked about it, Scheibe simply said it wasn't important.

At the end of the interview, the subject had to sign a three-page, fine print, legal release form. It released the experimenter, the experimenter's supervisors, the Massachusetts General Hospital, the State of Massachusetts, the National

Institute of Mental Health and the United States government from any and all consequences resulting from participating in this experiment.

Scheibe also mentioned, casually, that this was a "sensory deprivation" experiment. The term had been around in our culture for a while. Then the subject in the experimental group went into the same boring, but not soundproof, not darkened, treatment room that control group subjects had each sat in for two hours.

As you can imagine, the results were quite different. A number of experimental group subjects pressed the panic button. It got just too weird, they couldn't handle the full two hours! The questionnaire results basically showed that all of the psychotic-like effects associated with the actual reduction of sensory stimuli to the brain, real sensory deprivation, could be produced by suggestion alone. People talked about how their bodies felt like they were getting bigger and smaller, for example, some reported strange sensations of moving, unusual emotional states, movements of shadows, etc.

Scheibe and Orne demonstrated that all the effects attributed to a procedure on its presumed basic physiological function of cutting down actual sensory stimulation could be produced psychologically just by expectation. It certainly demonstrated to me that all of the sensory deprivation research needed to be done over again, realizing that it was not just that you were depriving people of sensory stimulation, you were doing it within a certain expectational context. Practically all sensory deprivation research had been done in hospitals, by psychiatrists, often with the implicit or explicit model that this might produce a result that would help us model something like what mental illness was. It was useful to learn from Scheibe and Orne's study that implicit expectations alone could pretty much produce all the phenomena erroneously attributed to sensory deprivation, but it undercut the supposedly sound conclusions and understandings of dozens of previous studies of sensory deprivation.

I said earlier that, ideally, we would have a group of totally unbiased people, with no expectations, practice meditation as a basic technique in developing a science of consciousness. But you can see from this example and many others I could give that this is much too simplistic a notion. We can try to understand bias and compensate for it or reduce it, but it's foolish to assume that it's not there at all.

Coming back, then, to our focus on developing a science of consciousness, of mind, you bring somebody in and teach them a meditation technique, but you must realize that people (almost) always come in with expectations. We scientists, we experimenters, also almost always have strong expectations that may affect our psychological work. Most experimenters not only have expectations, they communicate them to their subjects in various ways. Most experimenters also have an important, if noble, delusion that further complicates life, the delusion of objectivity. "I am an objective scientist, doing this research as an open-minded, unbiased search for the truth!" Even when an experimenter realizes that her subjects have important expectations, the attitude often tends to be something like "Well, subjects may have expectations, but that's noise, that's error variance, so you run a lot of subjects and it will average itself out."

The pervasiveness of unrecognized, systematic biases and expectations makes it very hard to set up a science of consciousness in a simple-minded way. We can't say we can somehow test people without expectations — unless you get somebody who is dead. They may come in with no expectations, but if they're dead, there is not much consciousness to study! So you must recognize the problem of bias and expectation, at both overt and subtle levels, and try to compensate for it.

This question of bias in experiments has always been of interest to me. Throughout my entire experimental career I've always said to myself that I would like to be an objective investigator, but I'm probably biased, so it would be a good idea if I figured out what my biases are — and then maybe I can compensate for them. As long as I maintain the delusion that I'm completely objective, my biases run in a totally uncontrolled fashion. So if we're going to develop a science of consciousness, we're going to have to take the expectations of both subjects and experimenters into account. Suppose somebody sits down to learn a meditation procedure; one person comes in because they think it will help them with their back pain; another person comes in because they think it will make them spiritual — whatever "spiritual" means to them; the third person comes in thinking it will increase their psychological insight; and so on.

One approach, a fairly traditional scientific one, is to assess the biases and expectations and try to see what effects different expectations have on what comes out of meditation procedures. That's a good approach.

We might also ask a really important question, however. Could the vipassana meditation technique eventually transcend all expectations? Allow us to see truth beyond our biases?

One of the more interesting results for me from doing vipassana, insight meditation, is that often some of the most important things I've learned from it are just what the expectations I brought to it are. I've sometimes had insights into the biases, the hopes, the fears, the expectations I've been bringing into meditation practice (or into my life generally) and which have been pushing my mind in certain directions. Sometimes as a result of seeing a bias or expectation, I can then drop it and get what seems like a clearer perception of reality. Sometimes the bias keeps right on working as soon as my attention drifts from seeing it, and it may take multiple insights into it before it stops running my life. To a certain extent it may be possible that this general technology of quieting the mind through concentrative meditation and then learning to pay clear, balanced attention may not only make biases more visible so you can see them, it might begin to enable us to overcome them.

So I think we have some possibilities for a science of consciousness that uses concentrative meditation, vipassana meditation and sensing, looking, and listening. I think we have possibilities to create a dedicated network of people who practice meditation, who are aware of biases, who eventually begin to see and filter out their biases, who begin pooling their knowledge, both observational and theoretical — and this may be a vital part of developing a real, Western science of consciousness. And such a science of consciousness could include state-specific work within various ASCs also. We don't have time to go into that today, but I've written extensively on my proposal for creating state-specific sciences elsewhere (Tart 1972) (Tart 1998), even though we're not quite, as a society, ready for that yet.

And now you can ask your too long delayed question, because that's the point at which my line of thinking stopped.

STUDENT: *Well, thank you, that does cover much more than my question. It looks like you're working on developing that kind of science of consciousness with us scientists who are part of this workshop today. You taught us some techniques for quieting and observing our minds, then you've asked us to report our resulting experiences. Several of us responded with first person narratives, "I experienced this and that," kinds of reports. But isn't there a bias in the scientific method itself which denies the validity of this kind of approach, which denigrates our reports of experience?*

Oh, yes. But note that the scientist part of me was not the primary part leading you through experiential exercises today. I'm biased in several ways when I do these workshops! I want people to have a good experience. At the same time, though, I don't want to fall into my old hypnosis researcher days where I just wanted to program particular experiences for people. So I try to strike some kind of balance between saying things which I think will be useful for a lot of people, while at the same time trying to minimize the degree to which I suggest specific experiences. But while we've talked a lot about science, I would not describe the kind of narratives people have reported here about what they experienced as "scientific" reports on it, unless I qualified them as initial, preliminary reports.

If I were trying to collect quality data, for instance, at a minimum, I should have had everybody write their reports in private and turn them in before group discussion, so you wouldn't have heard anybody else's and perhaps be influenced by them in writing your own. Then the biases I brought into the instructions would have to be teased out and their effects evaluated. I know I'm biased! So while I've talked about the importance of trained introspection, mindfulness, in developing a Western science of consciousness, we haven't made much of a start on it yet, including today, compared to what needs to be done.

Student: *My question wasn't to reinforce the idea of your bias, but rather to offer the challenge to most scientists that what you used today doesn't have to be regarded as biased. When a person says, "I see the rug that's right before my eyes, that I didn't see before, as a result of sensing, looking, and listening" and you say, "Yes it used to be just an old hotel rug, unnoticed, but now you see it as really is," to me that's data!*

I'd forgotten, I got caught up in conceptualizing . . . this really is an interesting rug, isn't it?

STUDENT: *Indeed! Now again, you see, now there is data.*

Yes.

STUDENT: *Why can science not regard this as a valid data? To put it another way, why do we have scientific dogmas that keep us from looking at this kind of data? How can we change that attitude, get past the dogma?*

You want me to wax sociological about the big why?

STUDENT: *No, I want you to change it to why not! What is your experience as a scientist in dealing with biases and dogma?*

Okay, you've tempted me and I'll succumb briefly, and reflect on this issue from forty-plus years of working in consciousness research, as it is important to the goal of establishing a science of consciousness. There is and has been tremendous bias against having a science of consciousness, against accepting consciousness *per se* into science at all. That's why I'm so thrilled that these Tucson meetings are happening: they are an incredible breakthrough compared to attitudes even a decade ago. So, why the biases?

For one thing, science generally has not known how to deal with the "hard" sciences. Now I deliberately use "hard" and "easy" in a different way than they are usually used. The easy sciences are things like physics, chemistry, and biology, all those areas of reality where your cultural background, personality and expectations don't make much difference. The hard, the difficult sciences are areas like psychology and psychiatry where you, the experimenter, may have a tremendous effect on what you observe. So, at a first level, what we'd like to have as a science of consciousness is a much tougher proposition to develop than in the more established kinds of physical sciences, which are the easy sciences by comparison.

As a second look at why we don't have more of a science of consciousness, I suspect a part of the reason — and those of you in the mental health professions will recognize this — is that a lot of people are not very comfortable with their own minds, and they don't want to look deeper. There is an attitude like "I've experienced enough suffering as it is! Leave well enough alone! I don't want to look in there! I don't trust what might be below the everyday surface of my mind!" So I think there is a significant level of dynamic, defensive resistance to developing a science of consciousness from many scientists' personal psychology.

Third, you have, of course, social fashion. Consciousness went out of style for a long while. I remember that when I was in graduate school I wanted to do my thesis and dissertation work on dreams. I was not getting too much encouragement on this from my faculty advisors, but they already knew I was stubborn, so they let me go ahead. But while I was reading the background literature I read a book by an English philosopher (Malcolm 1959) that *proved logically that there were no such things as dreams*! I had unpleasant dreams about this all night long!

But social and professional climates can change. As I was getting ready to do my thesis research, which, as I said, I was discouraged, but not prevented, from doing because dreams were "subjective" and therefore "unreal," psychologist and others began to discover a landmark article that Eugene Aserinsky and Nathaniel Kleitman had published in *Science* (Aserinsky 1953). They found that dreaming seemed to occur during a "real," *physiologically defined* EEG period at night. Presto! Overnight, dreams became real for the scientific community! Dreams got associated with something physical, and what was physical was real! That's the same thing that happened with meditation later. In the scientific and medical literature, meditation, when mentioned at all, was some sort of pathological, schizoid thing done by people in backward countries, and it was subjective and unreal. Then we had an article in *Science* (Wallace 1970) that showed that there were physiological changes, metabolic and EEG changes, associated with a meditation practice, Transcendental Meditation. Oh, meditation must be "real" after all!

On the social-political level, I appreciate these little episodes of legitimization that make things easier for people who want to research areas which had not been socially legitimate before. But in terms of coming up with a really adequate science of consciousness, it's a real drawback that we have to legitimatize these things by reducing them to the preferred belief system, physiology, materiality, the "mind is nothing but brain" dogma, explaining them "away." A part of the reason we're able to have this Tucson conference is that there has been a lot of progress made in understanding the brain, and a lot of progress made in developing psychoactive drugs that can have useful psychiatric benefits. This physiological progress has partially legitimized an interest in mind *per se*.

The other big thing that's changed the social scientific attitude about consciousness has been computers. Computers broke the "Don't try to look inside the box!" mentality that prevailed so long in psychology, the behaviorist attitude. If you're writing a computer program, you can't just say "Here's an input and here's an output, and that's the objectively observable behavior." You've got to figure out precisely why a computer "behaves" the way it does by matching or creating that behavior by writing a program to do that kind of thing.

Now my hope is that we won't get too caught up in the "explaining away" paradigm as an essential part of the legitimization process for consciousness research. This is the non-scientific faith that "The neurologists or biochemists will explain consciousness away someday as being *nothing but* certain electrical and chemical interactions between certain brain nuclei." This article of faith is non-scientific because it's a non-falsifiable hypothesis: you can't prove that someday they won't prove something! I hope that while we have this window of opportunity of a general, burgeoning interest in consciousness, such as these Tucson meetings express, we'll really look at consciousness *per se*.

My particular, working theoretical position is that I am an *interactive, pragmatic dualist*. Doesn't that sound "real" when I label it with all those big philosophical terms? My own research, and the research of other people that I respect, has convinced me that "mind" has a reality of its own that is inherently non-reducible to brain functioning. I mean non-reducible in a much stronger sense than just the systems theory sense that you have emergent properties that you can't reduce to simple additive interactions of subsystem actions. I mean non-reducible in that hard data shows that "mind" can do real things that no brains, or reasonable extrapolation of the properties of brains, can ever do, given our current scientific knowledge of the nature of physical reality and reasonable extensions of that knowledge. There is no reasonable doubt in my mind, for example, that paranormal phenomena like telepathy and clairvoyance happen sometimes — the experimental evidence is overwhelming. There is also no doubt in my mind that no reasonable, straightforward extensions of contemporary physics can explain those principles. Brains don't produce, by orders of magnitude, strong enough electromagnetic radiation, for example, to convey telepathic messages around the world, but such events do happen (see, e.g., (Broughton 1991) (Irwin 1994) (Radin 1997) for recent authoritative reviews and summaries of this evidence).

I know someone will raise the issue of quantum physics and consciousness. Some of my best friends are quantum physicists who say "We'll explain these paranormal effects with quantum physics someday." I wish them well, but in point of fact, in terms of demonstrable, measurable data, they've had very little success. I have an old-fashioned, essential scientific belief that a really good scientific understanding, a really good theory of something, leads to prediction and control of the phenomena. My friends and colleagues who are quantum physicists do parapsychology experiments, and get the same, statistically-significant-but-not-very-strong results that people who wouldn't know a quantum from a hole in the ground get. Their theoretical understanding is not manifested to the point of actually having any practical results yet. Perhaps it will someday, perhaps not. So maybe they are on to something, but maybe not.

I'm quite impressed by a highly prestigious scientific field like quantum physics, of course, and quite snowed by people who talk about it, but there are no impressive results yet when it comes to explaining parapsychological phenomena. And if there ever are impressive results, a "reduction" to quantum physics feels pretty different from the usual materialistic reductionism that has an explicit or implicit Newtonian solid-matter universe as its basis.

So I think it's vitally important to study mind in and of itself, because not only is that interesting, not only is that where we live, but I do think mind is something different than just the physiological structure of the brain and nervous system. I don't think I can sit back and wait in my studies because someday the neurophysiologists will explain it all for me.

STUDENT: *As a psychologist who's done so much work on consciousness and altered states that you will go down in the history books, perhaps you can clear up for me some things, like how hypnosis is a different form of consciousness, or the exact meaning of terms like hypnosis, self-conscious, unconscious, super-conscious, subconscious, and the collective unconscious. So would you comment a little bit on these, centered around the word conscious?*

All of those heady concepts, and such praise! Do you intend for this to go to my head?

STUDENT: *Yes!*

Give me the words again, one at a time. That was a long list and, as I said, memory is not my forte.

STUDENT: *Subconscious and unconscious.*

When I use the term *un*conscious I generally mean it in the Freudian sense, which to me is a very useful concept, a useful explanation for certain behaviors. Suppose, for example, you're interviewing someone about their relationships and they say, "I love my brother very much," but you note a certain angry tone and clenched muscles that don't seem to go along with strong, unalloyed feelings of love. But as far as you can tell, insofar as the person you're interviewing can accurately describe their conscious experience, they're talking about love. Yet anger is more than a simple reflex. So you've got to postulate processes somewhat like conscious processes that are goal directed, that are intelligent, but outside of ordinary waking consciousness and affecting behavior. That's how I use the term unconsciousness.

*Sub*conscious I generally use in a wider sense, to include a lot of positive potentials of processes outside of ordinary consciousness, as well as the Freudian unconscious. I think both these terms are generally used this way if used properly, but certainly there is a lot of sloppy use that confuses the issue.

Did that get all of that, or was there another word?

STUDENT: *The collective unconscious.*

The collective unconscious is a term coined by Carl Jung. Jung sometimes noticed that material he attributed to his patients' unconscious minds, dream material or visionary material, showed a remarkable resemblance to little known myths (Jung himself was quite knowledgeable about such material) from other, often dead, cultures. A Swiss patient, for example, might have a very emotionally powerful dream about a living Sun with many hands reaching out from it. So how would an ordinary layperson raised in Switzerland come up with classic Egyptian religious symbolism, from a culture which vanished thousands of years ago? I haven't been to Switzerland, except to pass through an airport, but they tell me the Swiss are very conservative, thoroughly Western people who are not involved in sun worship and things like that! Yet Jung saw too much of this sort of symbolism to dismiss it as mere coincidence, so he postulated that every human's mind has, at a level even deeper than their personal unconscious, a collective unconscious, a stratum of mind that is common to all humans. Under certain unusual circumstances, like dreaming, psychosis, etc., products of this mind, archetypes of the collective unconscious, manifest in consciousness in spite of lack of obvious cultural connection or conscious knowledge.

Many psychologists have thought this was a very improbable theory. How could a mental experience be inherited across centuries and cultures? But the idea of a collective unconscious has never seemed that improbable to me. Even staying within a strictly physiological, mind = brain framework, if your genes can pass along instructions as to how to build and operate a kidney, for example, why can't they pass along instructions for certain psychological experiences that will manifest under certain circumstances? I can see the collective unconscious as genetically transmitted, analogous to read-only memory in your computer. Every computer, in addition to the programs you load in as software (analogous to what you're taught in life by the world and others), has some programs, some instructions, encoded in the BIOS, the Basic Input Output System, that are analogous to experiences biologically preprogrammed into the collective unconscious. I've mentioned earlier that I'm a pragmatic, interactive dualist, but that does not conflict with this idea that the hardware side of consciousness, the brain, can have genetically transmitted programs in it that, if activated, produce certain kinds of psychological experiences.

This is a fairly conventional way of looking at the idea of the collective unconscious. That may not be the whole story, though. It may also be, as some people think and I'm open to, some kind of independently existent realm of mind that it's possible for human beings to tap into. Contents of the collective unconscious may also be independently existing aspects of this mind reality that can be tapped into because they are there, "real," even if they weren't taught to you in the enculturation process.

STUDENT: *Superconscious?*

Superconscious is not a word I generally use because I find it too vague. It covers an awful lot of things; it's something of a general catchall category for all sorts of things that seem to fit in the category of extraordinary mental functioning. I suppose we need a catchall term like that. Exceptional human abilities or exceptional human experiences (EHEs) would be a good term for this wide spectrum. You ought to go to Rhea White's workshop on Exceptional Human Experiences tomorrow (http://www.ehe.org/). She's built up quite a database now on a wide variety of EHEs people have, as well as coining the term.

When I talk about the sorts of things I think people would lump under the term superconscious, I tend to try to figure out whether there were specific ASCs involved. But ASCs cover a wide range of patterns of functioning, which are both "super" and "sub," which are a mixture of better and worse functioning in specific ways, compared to ordinary consciousness functioning. ASCs are like ordinary consciousness, really, which has its good points and its bad points.

STUDENT: *Well then supra-consciousness, I don't even know what that means necessarily, but . . . ?*

If you don't know what it means, I don't know what it means either! No. I won't talk about supra-consciousness. The fact that we have a word like supra-consciousness means somebody's enthusiastic about the potentialities of mind, but it's not a common or clearly defined word.

STUDENT: *The potentials of mind are clearly really important, but, on the other hand, the way that I've learned sciences and methodology, the first thing that you have to do is to define your terms. If you can't even define what consciousness is and what mind is, aren't we going towards the realm of religion which is kind of like, well I can't tell you what it is, but it isn't science, and I really think it's important to know.*

Okay, good issue. We're coming from different schools as our primary background. To me, the absolutely primary defining characteristic of science is to discover, refine and work with the *data*. The intellectual superstructure, which means, by definition, concepts that you put on top of the data, is the secondary activity.

Now when you practice essential science, the way I've described it earlier, you sometimes reach a point where a theory comes along that works really, really well. It accounts for (almost) all of the data you think is important in your field, it makes excellent, validated predictions, and it also indicates what lines of further work are needed to refine things. You have gotten a *paradigm*. It feels like you've finally discovered the basic truths about why things work the way they do in your field. Psychologically, you have a *law* of gravity, for example, rather than a theory of gravity. It's a great feeling of accomplishment for people in a field when they reach that stage.

As we briefly discussed earlier, Thomas Kuhn (Kuhn 1962) called a field's activity after this point *paradigmatic science*, or "normal" science. "Normal" because most fields recognized as sciences today have such a paradigm as a result of their long history. Practitioners of the field now take the intellectual superstructure as primary. Practitioners now tend to automatically and somewhat unthinkingly say, for example, that certain research is "obviously" not important to do because it's about a "trivial" effect or no effect all. Certain things become, psychologically, a priori impossible, and if anyone claims there is data for such "impossible" effects, that person and their data is prejudicially dismissed without "wasting time" investigating. The data of scientific parapsychology are an excellent case study of prejudicial, paradigmatic social effects that hinder essential science (Hess 1992) (Hess 1993) (Martin 1998).

STUDENT: *Do you think our ordinary minds substitutes concepts for perceptions then?*

Most of the time.

STUDENT: *It's frustrating! There are all these complications about consciousness, taking our beliefs for the facts and the like. But we're talking about consciousness and mind, yet can't define it. How do we know that we're conversing about the same thing?*

We know, to a reasonable, not absolute, degree of certainty that we're conversing about the same thing by talking with each other in more detail, working out consequences from what we think we've understood and communicated successfully in our talking, and seeing if the predicted and observable consequences agree. To put it in terms of essential science, we each have our internal, individual theory of what we're talking about and communicating, then we make predictions of consequences to each other. To the degree that our communication of what we can observe about these consequences agrees with each other, it's reasonable to conclude we're communicating, that our individual, internal understandings have a good match with each other.

There many aspects of consciousness that are indeed extremely difficult to describe verbally. We have a word for it: ineffable experiences. Strangely enough, we don't talk about "effable" experiences, but we certainly have ineffable experiences!

STUDENT: *Physicists can talk about the speed of light, but it's like we're trying to talk about the speed of dark!*

The speed of dark? That's very good!

We do have to be careful in our attempts to communicate about consciousness. Many times, for instance, people come to me to tell me about ASC experiences they've had. Generally I'll just listen at first, hopefully without interrupting (a bad habit of mine), and let them tell it their way. After they're done, I'll recognize that there are parts (or perhaps the whole) of what they've described that I think I understand. "Understand" in the sense that my personal experience has apparently been like some aspects of what they've described, so I'm assuming their experience was like mine. So even though those aspects may be ineffable, difficult to put in words, I assume that by consulting my own memories of that kind of experience that I have a good understanding of what they're trying to tell me. As a more ordinary parallel, if someone says "Look at that cat over there," I know from my own experience what cats are like and have a good chance of seeing what's she's referring to.

I don't *know* in any absolute sense, but I'm assuming this forms an initial basis of communication. For some of the other things they describe about their experience, I may recognize that I don't have any clear idea what they're talking about. Now sometimes it's easy to recognize that we're not communicating well because they'll keep saying things like, "I don't know how to express this," and/or say a bunch of contradictory things, so we're in one hundred percent agreement that I don't understand. Other times they'll say something, the words are familiar, my mind wants to put it into a familiar pattern so I'll think I understand, but some part of me says, "Ah, I may be being misled by the familiarity of the words here and/or my desire to believe I understand. Better be careful in thinking I understand!"

Part of the problem in communicating about consciousness, ordinary or altered, is that we have a bias such that we all want to be accepted and form bonds with each other. We all like to think we understand each other, so we have a tendency to gloss over lack of understanding. That's good for forming friendships — up to a point. It's not good for scientific investigation.

One of the things I've learned if I want to try to understand people's ASC experiences is to focus on what I clearly don't understand, but then, even more importantly, to be careful with the parts I think I understand! The usual way I try to test my understanding of such parts is say them back to the reporter in a different form, perhaps using several different analogies which all should express the same principle if I actually understand. If I do understand it, they'll probably agree with my version that's altered in form but, hopefully, not in essence. For example, let's drop back in time to the 60s and 70s and somebody tells me they experienced "vibes," in some altered state. Maybe "good vibes, " maybe "bad vibes." I'll listen and then what I'll usually do is ask something like "Okay, if I understand you correctly, you experienced something going back and forth?" I'm assuming "vibes," vibrations is being used in a literal sense as a first try. Sometimes they'll say

"Yes," but sometimes they'll say "Well no, that's not what I meant by vibes, I meant such-and-such." So I don't know if I can come to any absolute understanding, but I feel I can come to a clearer understanding through dialogue of what that person has experienced.

The usefulness of trying to understand consciousness through communication like this depends, of course, on my own repertoire of experiences. To the extent that my consciousness has had only a narrow range of life experiences, consciousness experiences, I think I'll be less able to understand experiences outside that range. Thus part of the training for a scientist of consciousness is to have a wide range of experiences.

STUDENT: *Do you want to put some positive things in the Freudian unconscious too? Is that all right?*

My personal, as well as professional, approach tends to be that I see a certain degree of truth in everybody's theory of consciousness. Where I get off the boat is when any one of them says "Now, with my theory, you have the complete account of what consciousness is all about." So yes, there is a lot of useful material in the Freudian theory of the unconscious.

Where I thought you were going to go in your question, which you didn't, was the idea that perhaps some aspects of unconscious activity are inherently not understandable by consciousness, even if they could ever be made conscious. I know Freud postulated that. And it might be true. But, of course, if we believe in such limits a priori, we won't try to transcend them! So some aspects of consciousness will remain non-understandable. That's a trivial example of being trapped by our own biases, not a truth about those aspects of consciousness, though.

STUDENT: *Freud did talk about some things being repressed, so they weren't expressed in a way that made sense to consciousness.*

Right, but it's more than expression or lack of it, it's just that they're not comprehensible to consciousness *per se*. We're speculating about things that are inherently incomprehensible. But see that involves a degree of humility most of us don't like to have. I prefer to believe that potentially I am capable of understanding everything! But I'm not sure how much I totally believe that. It may very well be that there are some things you can't comprehend.

How many of you have ever read any of Carlos Castaneda's books about his Yaqui Indian teacher, the shaman don Juan (see, e.g. (Castaneda 1968))? (*Many hands go up.*)

In don Juan's cosmology — and please don't ask me whether don Juan was real or not, but he was sure a real interesting character, whether Castaneda made him up or whether he was real! — the universe was divided into three realms of experience. One was everyday, understandable experience. People knew that kind of stuff. The second was experiences that seemed "magical" or mysterious or "mystical" or incomprehensible to the ordinary person, but a properly trained mind could learn to grasp and use them. They had their own inherent logic and lawfulness, and a human being could learn that. But then don Juan added a third category of potential experience: things that could be experienced but could never be understood by a human being. They were outside of what a human mind had the capacity to cope with. Don Juan added the admonition to try to stay out of that realm; it would just drive you nuts! You can't understand it, it's your nature as a human not to be able to understand it. How would you distinguish between the two latter categories? That might be hard.

The Buddha drew a somewhat similar kind of distinction, although his was conditional. There is a list in the Buddhist literature of several phenomena of which he said, in effect, don't waste your time thinking about these until you get fully enlightened. They're absolutely impossible for anything less than a fully enlightened mind to understand, and thinking about them before you get fully enlightened will not only be unprofitable, it will drive you crazy!

These Four Imponderables, as they are called, are (1) the full complexity of karma, (2) questions about how and why existence all started, (3) the range of the mind in the advanced meditative, concentrative states of samadhi, and (4) the range of the fully enlightened Buddha mind.

STUDENT: *Aren't we coming here to a point or dimension of semantic and linguistic confusion? The words can affect how we think about things.*

Probably! Part of that dimension, too, is whether you are using language to communicate, or using it to manipulate? Are you trying to get people to discover things on their own, or are you trying to tell them the way things are? Those are very real dimensions.

Let me give you an example, going back to Shinzen Young. I first met him at a scientific conference in 1986 where he gave a lecture on meditation. I found his lecture extremely interesting, because a part of me kept saying, "This man is talking from actual experience!" I realized I had heard Eastern-born meditation teachers talk about similar things, and they spoke very well about meditation, but now I realized that for some (maybe most) of those people I didn't know whether they had actually experienced the things they were talking about, or whether they were just the inheritors of a "line," a collection of lectures that had been polished for a couple of thousand years now and were really well phrased. Clearly when someone is speaking about the ineffable, their hope of genuinely communicating what is vital is going to be greatly affected by whether they speak from actual personal experience or only from "theory," from polished, but second-hand, teachings.

I've come to realize over the years that any teacher may be trying very hard to help you learn the tools to discover things about the mind on your own, but, at the same time, inadvertently manipulating, biasing you to experience things in certain ways. Shinzen works hard to teach the tools, but some of the other teachers I've heard over the years are more involved with shaping what you might experience.

Now, thinking of experience, I have to ask a question. We have a little over an hour left. Do we want to go on in a general discussion vein here, or would you like me to take back through some of these meditation exercises to give you a little more drill in doing it?

STUDENT: *More drill!*

ANOTHER STUDENT: *Why don't you add movement to the meditation exercises?*

Why don't I add movement to the meditation exercises? It can be done. There are some practical limitations on our setting today, though, the room is cramped and our time is short. So what else could we do?

STUDENT: *We could go into the theory of meditation more deeply.*

Okay, I'd like to do that! You know I am a thoughtaholic, though, so I'm trying to abstain a little bit and we should focus on more practice, perhaps expanding the practice some.

STUDENT: *One question before we set out to new terrain. Could the use of psychedelic drugs perhaps be a way to initiate a person into meditation, or be a tool to, say, deepen meditative insights?*

Yes, used properly.

STUDENT: *I'm not thinking about amphetamines, but certain psychedelics that you have researched that seem like they would be useful.*

Well, let me put it this way. Ignoring the reality of illegality for the moment — any reality is easy for theoreticians to ignore — let's imagine we lived in a more perfect social reality, where there is properly done psychedelic research and applications, under safe and legal auspices.

I'm convinced that the primary action of a psychedelic drug — something like LSD or mescaline for instance — is to interfere with neural processes that construct reality in the habitual form that you're used to having it constructed in (Tart 1975). It basically throws monkey wrenches (partly at random) into the gears of the neural and psychological machinery, as it were, and so the gears slip and lock, speed up and slow down, in funny ways. I'm speaking now from my whole systems approach to ordinary and altered stated of consciousness, which views (states of) consciousness as bio-psychological virtual reality devices, as world simulation processes. Sometimes the result of that slippage is that habitual mental and brain processes that block clear and accurate perception are temporarily inhibited, and a person gets a clearer, truer, more valid view of important things in life. Mixed in with that, sometimes these monkey wrenches in the gears make the gears turn faster and illusions now acquire a tremendous reality, a "This is The Truth beyond doubt!" quality that they never had before. So what a psychedelic does, in an untrained person in our particular cultural setting, is both increase glimpses of truth and increase the intensity of illusions. This is a heady mixture, and the person who had the experience then has the task of trying to sort it out later on.

I'll give you an example. In the early days of research with LSD, when the distinction between "psychotomimetics" (mimicking the action of a psychosis) and "psychedelics" (mind-manifesting, allowing both positive and negative aspects of the mind to be experienced), began to be made, some people began to realize that yes, the set and setting that these drugs were given in probably had a big effect on what actually happened. A couple of psychiatrists decided they wanted to get into research on these drugs, but there was already a growing and heated controversy among people who said "No researcher should ever take any of these drugs themselves, because then they will have permanent holes in their brain and would be totally unreliable!" (not to mention disturbing the social status differences between "researchers" and "subjects") versus those who said "Researchers who have not actually had this experience themselves cannot possibly understand what it's really about, and their research will be shallow and irrelevant." Damned if you did and damned if you didn't!

So these two psychiatrists decided they would "compromise." One of them would take a psychedelic and the other wouldn't, and then they'd work later as a research team, hopefully combining the best of both worlds. So they flipped a coin and one of them took a psychedelic.

I've often been asked whether the "winner" or the "loser" of the toss got to take the psychedelic, but I don't quite know how they structured it! The form of the question says a lot.

The psychiatrist who took the psychedelic was in a small room near the main laboratory when he had what was absolutely convincingly to him a "mystical experience" of The Truth. Engraved on a plaque on the wall were words that revealed all the truth a human being needed to know in life! Everything you needed to live the good life was revealed! As you can imagine, he was ecstatically happy at having made this discovery!

The words were, "Please flush after using."

Now, having been a subject myself in psychedelic experiments, I can kind of appreciate that, all right? I can draw on old memories to see how you could get into that saying, and you could find a lot of wisdom there. And yet, somehow . . . I suspect that probably not *all* the wisdom of the Universe was encapsulated in that one saying! There are a few other things you need to know to live the good life.

So I think psychedelics are a lot like that, a mix of "better truth" and more intense delusion that can be hard to sort out. Now if *properly trained* people used psychedelics, it would probably be a whole different ballgame. Shamanic use of psychedelics, for instance, in traditional cultures where this has been done for a long time, is not at all the same as some sixteen-year-old Western kid on a "trip." The shaman not only needs to have unusual experiences, they must be socially useful in the long run, or the community's not going to support such practices. "I paid you to do this shamanic work because I needed you to find my lost cow, and you didn't find the lost cow! I'm not giving you any more business!" There is a discipline and prolonged training brought to the use of psychedelics for their effect on consciousness in some traditional cultures which we understand very little about, and which we certainly don't have within our culture.

STUDENT: *In the 60s it happened differently. In the 60s it flowed differently then, we had validation of psychedelic research by the government, then invalidation as a result of overzealous psychedelic researchers. These things, do you think, a futile question, I know, but would we be interested in the question of meditation if psychedelic research had continued on track without blinders? Did that psychedelic research make any difference?*

It certainly made a difference for me! As I said earlier, I was a subject in experiments with psychedelic drugs while I was in graduate school, and as a result it took theoretical knowledge and ideas I had about many aspects of consciousness and gave me a direct, experiential knowledge base for them that tremendously stimulated my own interest in the mind.

Now, given what I said about investigators' biases earlier, you understand that some people think I have a permanent hole in my head, so, if they are right, you mustn't take any of what I say too seriously! Even more fun, in a political sense, is that I eventually discovered that the psychiatric experiments I was a subject in were covertly bankrolled by the CIA through one of its front foundations, so I can honestly say that when I was a young and impressionable fellow, the CIA gave me powerful psychedelic drugs, so I'm not responsible for anything I say or do! Can't I sue somebody? I think I ought to send them a thank-you letter, actually; it was extremely interesting and enlightening!

Now let's tie this in with the meditation context. I know some Buddhist teachers who, when they were young back in the 60s and 70s, took psychedelics, and they've told me that those experiences turned their attention to trying to better understand the mind and use it more effectively. But when they discovered classical Buddhist meditation and developed some skill at it, they felt they had discovered what they considered a more powerful and reliable tool. Yes, the psychedelics might have given them "previews" — it was like going to the movies and seeing a documentary on, say, how to build a dam and irrigation system, so you can grow more crops for your village. But going back and seeing the preview over and over again doesn't build a dam! The movie may be exciting and it may be glorious Technicolor and whatnot, very exhilarating to see the movie, but you've got to learn a lot of technical skills about how to build a dam and then actually do the hard work to apply the knowledge if that's what you want to do.

So these people became meditation students and eventually meditation teachers, for they found meditation far more reliable. The Buddhist tradition also is anti-drug in a sense that Buddhist thinking about the human condition is that we suffer (uselessly) because we're already under the control of a million external (to the mind) things, and if we're looking for freedom and enlightenment, we have to be able to develop total control over our own minds. If you have to get your pleasure and insights through an external agent, like a drug, then you're dependent on something external to yourself, you're not totally free. So the traditional discipline rules of Buddhism forbid intoxicating drugs if you really want to get somewhere. There is some variation from culture to culture, of course, and some argument as to whether it's an absolute prohibition against "intoxicating" drugs *per se* or a prohibition against using such drugs to the point where they seriously interfere with mental functioning.

But my best guess is that in an "ideal" world, some people could benefit in many ways, meditatively, as an adjunct to psychotherapy and growth methods, religiously, philosophically, etc., from *properly used* psychedelics. I think I did. I think I was, metaphorically speaking, hit over the head with a very powerful blow that called my attention to aspects of mind I might never have noticed otherwise, or would only have had some interesting words about. So I look back on my psychedelic experiences as very useful.

I've got no personal use for them now. Now I think, "Put some drug in my body and temporarily go crazy? What a scary, unappealing thing to do!" But hey, I was in my twenties back then, now I'm a lot more conservative, perhaps an old fart!

STUDENT: *Do you know Richard Alpert, the Harvard professor who got involved in psychedelic research and then got fired from Harvard for promoting psychedelic use? Didn't he change his name to Baba Ram Das or something like that?*

We had lunch together once when he was still a professor at Harvard. We spoke of research design and all those scientifically respectable things. It was an interesting lunch, and I've seen him occasionally in recent years. He's a more interesting person as Ram Das, I must say, then when he was a Harvard professor!

STUDENT: *Do you suppose that anyone ever learned how to dwell in self-remembering by taking psychedelics?*

Probably not. I suspect not because, again, self-remembering, sensing, looking, and listening, as I understand it, is a slightly "forced" technique. It produces an opening of consciousness that gives you a variety of insights and consequently alternative choices, but self-remembering comes from making this little but deliberate effort, not from having something imposed on you from the "outside" like a drug. Psychedelics sometimes may produce some effects that are similar to what can occur as a result of self-remembering, but the general pattern of effects is not the same.

We usually think of taking a psychoactive drug as done in the pursuit of pleasure, too, although serious growth and therapeutic usage can be more open. But one of the cautions I give people who are serious about self-remembering is that in doing this, sometimes you'll be much more clearly present to what a dog turd you are in life! Hang in there anyway, I admonish! Stay present!

Sometimes by being clearly present you have really special and positive experiences, so you'll start to think, "Well, this is it! I have arrived!" and you'll then start to forget to actually stay with the practice. Remember our Zen student who had the wonderful experiences, but forgot to focus on his breathing? The point is *to keep doing the practice, rather than getting sidetracked by any particular experience*, whether it's a "good" experience or a "bad" experience. The point is to keep making the commitment to pay clear attention to what is actually going on, *here, now*. That long term cultivation of awareness and self-remembering will make changes far more important than any temporary experience.

I want to emphasize something. The *self-remembering exercise is not a matter of sensing your body and feeling good*. That's not the point of it, and if you think that's the point of it, you can not only waste your time developing more satisfying daydreams, it can even be fatal. One of my teachers told me of an incident where a student of his, after a meeting, was standing out on the street, talking to other students, telling them how good she felt sensing her body and all the life in her body — and as she was talking and walking backwards, feeling the good sensations inside her body, a taxi ran her down and killed her. Too much attention given to sensing, not enough to looking and listening.

To sense, look, and listen, you deliberately, actively spread your attention around. You're looking at the world you live in, listening to the world you live in, and paying attention to your body. The goal is to become clearer about *everything* that's happening. If you're eating, additionally give lots of attention to tasting and smelling. If you're touching, give lots of attention to the sensations arising from touch.

I describe the self-remembering process as "sensing, looking, and listening" because sight and hearing are almost always our predominant senses, and we're deliberately adding keeping track of arm and leg sensations. Looking and listening is where we're taking in most of our information about the world. But the point of sensing, looking, and listening is not to feel good. It will make you feel generally good, generally more alive and vital, in the long run. But the more important purpose of sensing, looking, and listening is to develop better contact with reality.

That will mean that sometimes you'll see aspects of reality that are very unpleasant, and you'll see them more clearly than you normally see. That's not usually considered a plus from our ordinary perspective, which is one of the reasons we don't do this, why we don't pay much quality, open-minded attention to our selves and our world. We don't like to see negative things in the world or ourselves, so we run our little programs and get lost in our dreams and tune out. Remember Gurdjieff's saying, "Man is asleep!" But that sleep, the automatized, consensus trance state causes lots of trouble, either immediately or later on.

So, feeling good is nice but if you practice sensing, looking, and listening and one day it feels very good, you have to be real careful because that's a dangerous point. You may then subtly distort your understanding of what to do in order to try to reproduce the good feeling. *The self-remembering exercise is an exercise in getting closer to truth. Happiness is secondary.*

This is a hard point for us to take really seriously, because we're Americans. We're entitled to the pursuit of happiness, aren't we? Maybe even entitled to happiness *per se* and we ought to sue somebody if we don't get it? But I've become convinced that pursuit of happiness will lead you to a lot of

(unnecessary) suffering, because it's too easy to start psychologically distorting your perceptions in order to make yourself feel happy. If you don't see or hear things that would bother you, then you think you don't feel them. This is suppression and repression in action. If your thoughts and associated feelings run in automatized grooves that produce internal feelings of pleasure, you feel good and have less energy that might be attracted into noticing something unpleasant. But then you're getting out of touch with what's actually going on, and there will eventually be bad consequences. What I've found, though, is that *if you pursue truth and greater awareness to the best of your ability, happiness will come as a side effect*, without the reactive consequences that come from (pseudo-) happiness resulting from ignorance and unawareness.

STUDENT: *I've heard that lots of the people who are serious about meditation and any kind of spiritual growth got their start from psychedelic experiences. Is that true?*

There are virtually no actual data on that, but there are a lot of anecdotes that circulate around the various communities. About the only systematic data I can think of offhand is something I collected myself some years ago. I took a Tibetan Buddhist group that I was studying with, so that I was accepted as somebody that they could trust, and did a survey of previous psychedelic use (Tart 1991). I found an enormously high frequency of previous psychedelic use among students of this particular branch of Tibetan Buddhism. That's some of the most systematic data around, yet it's only a drop in the bucket in terms of the enormous number of people involved in spiritual growth disciplines, so there is no firm answer to your question.

STUDENT: *I've heard occasional stories in the meditation community that people who are already experienced meditators don't find psychedelic drugs very interesting when they try them.*

You're saying that meditation makes psychedelics have less effect on a person?

STUDENT: *Yes.*

I've heard some stories to that same effect, yes. I think a survey might concretize those stories and lab experiments might demonstrate that. If it's true, why? That would be real interesting to know why.

STUDENT: *You're indulging your addiction.*

You're right! Too much talk, not enough practice! I've been thinking about it in the back of my mind while we've talked: you guys are all enablers! Let's take a five-minute break, and then we're going to have an experience.

(break)

STUDENT: *Can you tell us about meditation with special sounds and chants? I think Transcendental Meditation is like that. How does that fit it with what you've taught us today?*

You're going to make me indulge again?

STUDENT: *Yes, just for a minute, I want to know what you think.*

Okay, mantra meditation, how it fits in. I've briefly mentioned Transcendental Meditation (TM), which is a form of mantra meditation, earlier, but it will be good to look at it in a little more detail.

A mantra is a sound, or internal representation of a sound, that you take for your focus point in meditation. Mantra meditation is usually considered a concentrative form of meditation. You have one thing you keep bringing your attention back to over and over. The way the TM people teach it, however, you do the mantra and if your mind wanders, don't get too uptight about its wandering, because, they teach, it has a reason to wander. Material will bubble up into awareness that needs to bubble up, and, when you feel a certain sense of completeness of that, which is probably about when you remember that you've lost the mantra, then you come back to the mantra. So it has the concentrative element, but TM has a certain insight element too.

Don't go away from our time together with the belief that

this classification scheme of concentrative and insight meditation is going to cover all the kinds of practices that are called meditation. Reality is always more complicated than our concepts about it.

CHAPTER **10**

Practice:
Vipassana to Self-Remembering

O kay, we're going to do a few minutes of concentrative meditation, then a few minutes of vipassana, which will then lead into the self-remembering practice in a little more active form than we've been doing it so far, so it should get interesting.

Settle yourself down . . .

Either close or park your eyes . . . and bring your attention down to the sensation of breathing in your belly and chest . . . as your abdomen moves in and out . . .

Take a minute to settle down if you need it . . .

Just let your attention rest on the sensation of breathing . . .

If your mind wanders . . . just gently bring it back . . .

Now you're concentrating on the sensation of breathing . . . but you're not deaf . . . so you do hear other sounds occasionally . . . If your eyes are open, you're not blind . . . so you do see other things occasionally . . . but the bulk of your attention . . . the focus of your attention . . . is on the breath.

Now expand your focus to just follow whatever sensations

there are in your body . . . You can follow the main sensation . . . or the more general pattern of sensations . . . or just open your mind, moment-by-moment, to what is, in terms of body sensation . . .

Now again, you're not deaf so you hear the outside sounds that comes through the walls or windows or doorways . . . but your primary focus is on opening your mind, to be really open to and to follow what the main sensations are that are happening in your body . . . the main sensations . . .

Now switch your focus so that your arms and legs . . . are the main focus of attention . . . and just follow whatever sensations . . . or patterns of sensations . . . occur in your arms and legs.

Now deliberately *expand* your focus to simultaneously listen to the quality of sounds . . . while sensing your arms and legs.

While continuing to listen to whatever sounds there are . . . and sensing your arms and legs . . . look around actively . . . If your eyes aren't already open, open them now . . . and look around . . . Look at each thing with fresh curiosity, like you've never seen it before . . .

Now I'm going to ask you to do some moving about in a minute . . . and I would like you to move a little bit slower than normal . . . so that you can keep in touch with the sensations in your arms and legs . . . and whatever other sensations are generated by movement in your body . . . as well as listening and looking . . . So move maybe ten percent or so slower than normal.

What I want you to do is *slowly* get up . . . and find a partner . . . preferably somebody you don't know . . . and sit down, so the two of you are side by side . . . No talking in the process, please, just really concentrate as fully as you can on feeling the sensations in your arms and legs and in your body from the movement . . . and on listening and looking . . .

So find a partner that way . . . When you've found one, sit

down, so everybody will be able to find one . . .

I'm going to have you interact with another living human being, which is always a big deal psychologically . . . but this is a special experimental and experiential situation . . . where your job is to be as clearly aware as possible . . .

The first part of this exercise involves making an intellectual decision, while still trying to sense, look, and listen . . . That is to decide which of you is the A partner, and which is the B partner . . . People get to reverse roles after a while, so it doesn't really make much difference who is A and who is B . . .

Okay, I assume that decision has been made . . . Now, while continuing to sense, look, and listen, A partner, give one of your hands to your B partner . . . B partner, take that hand . . . and examine it . . . like you've never seen a hand before . . . and continue to sense, look, and listen. Again, look at your partner's hand, with an open, curious mind, like you've never seen an object like this before . . .

If your mind has wandered, gently bring it back . . .

Okay, a few minutes have gone by . . . We will switch roles now, while continuing to sense, look, and listen . . . B partner, give one of your hands to your partner . . . A partner, keep sensing, looking, and listening, but examine that hand . . . being open to whatever it is like . . .

If your mind has wandered, gently bring it back . . .

Everybody continue to sense, look, and listen as I give you further instructions . . .

In this next exercise, you're going to have to sense, look, and listen even harder . . . You're going to have to really focus on it, because I'm going to have you talk . . . while continuing to sense, look, and listen . . . which might seem a difficult action . . . but *it can be done* . . . you can talk while you sense, look, and listen . . .

Now, A partner, you are going to talk for about two minutes or so to your B partner . . . telling your partner about yourself. B partner, your task is to look at your A partner and listen to what he or she says, and to sense your arms and legs as you listen . . . But it's very important that *you*, B partner, remain absolutely neutral as you listen . . . No nods, no smiles, no words, none of the usual social actions and responses that are expected in a conversation, or in listening . . . You really pay attention and listen, but you make no overt responses *of any sort* while your partner is talking.

A partner, you can talk about anything you want about yourself . . . you can introduce yourself . . . but, of course, try to sense, look, and listen while you talk . . . Go ahead . . .

If your mind has wandered, gently bring it back . . .

Okay, it's been a few minutes, reverse roles . . . Slowly and mindfully, while sensing, looking, and listening . . . B partner, you talk about yourself while your partner senses, looks, and listens, while making no overt responses . . .

Now slowly and mindfully . . . with both of you sensing, looking, and listening, I'd like you to stand up . . . shake hands with your partner . . . but actually pay attention to what you're doing, instead of the usual automatic handshake . . . and then quietly go back to your seat . . .

Be aware of the quality of attention in the room . . .

Okay, continue to sense, look, and listen, but we'll go back to a more "normal" talking mode now.

(Quality of strong attentiveness, focus and openness in room, difficult to describe)

CHAPTER 11

Taking the Practices Into Life

N ow I feel I've gotten you badly prepared for the rest of
the Tucson III conference, because it's not going to stay
like this!

There is something inherently satisfying about coming
more to the present, coming more to your senses. There is
something more "intelligent" about it in a quiet kind of way,
and I think practically everyone here has now had a taste of
some of the possibilities of mindfulness, of self-remembering.
That's very satisfying!

As I said earlier, it's really ridiculous to try to introduce
people to the techniques of mindfulness in a single day. In a
traditional way of training in meditation, you would get an
hour of practicing, meditating, to every five minutes of talk,
but you're all enablers of my thoughtaholism, and this is the
right kind of setting for our mutual addiction, so you've gotten a lot of explanation. Whether that's a more effective way
to teach, I don't know. I hope so, at least for people like us, but

it's certainly not the traditional way. But the traditional way wasn't a feasible one for our situation here, where I couldn't assume a common background, a common previous knowledge of meditation, or having a lot of time available.

I've introduced you to concentrative meditation, with the rationale that our mind is ordinarily too much out of control, bouncing about too wildly, and that causes a lot of problems, so we need to learn something to stabilize it.

I've introduced you to vipassana, "insight" or "opening up" meditation, where, having achieved (or achieving through future practice of concentrative meditation) some degree of stability, you begin to look into the workings of your mind, though not by the traditional way of training you to good stability in concentrative meditation first. We went right for it, due to our lack of time together. You began to look at a wider spectrum of experiences with an essentially scientific attitude of "What *is* happening, *here, now*?" You've looked with an attitude of "What *exactly* is happening?" rather than getting caught up in your theories about what *should* be happening, or what *was* happening, or what *might* be happening in the future.

I've introduced you to this self-remembering procedure of sensing, looking, and listening to bring this attitude of closer, open-minded attentiveness into a more active style of life. I haven't made our self-remembering practice very active simply because there is no time to really train in that kind of thing today. I see no point in making it complex enough to maybe have big failure experiences. But, in principle, you can maintain this attitude of self-remembering, of sensing, looking, and listening, this deliberate deployment of your attention to the body and to your senses to keep you in the present, in the rest of your life, even when you talk. I didn't think being mindful when I talked was possible when I first heard about it, but I've learned that it is possible.

If you continue to practice sensing, looking, and listening, you will find, as I hinted at earlier, that even though in some ways you may feel you are paying less attention to someone, because you're working on your own internal exercise, you'll probably actually have more accurate perceptions of that person, and eventually be considered a more responsive and caring person! Too much of our interaction with each other is two people getting off on their internal fantasies, and only peripherally interacting.

I've also mentioned something about the food of impressions. If you practice any formal meditations or this self-remembering regularly, your experiential diet is going to improve. I can't detail it, but there will be indirect ways in which your health and the quality of your life will get better, even without your trying for any specific changes in your life.

And then — I should say of course, for a bunch of thought-aholics like us! — in addition to this main meal of actual practice, we've had a great deal of intellectual seasoning, which might have been a distraction or which might have been essential. It's hard for me to tell how our day was for each of you, but you can tell, and I have my suspicions, judging from my perceptions of you and the content of your questions, that it worked out very nicely. You've gotten the taste I wanted to give you.

My suggestion is that after you leave our workshop today, you deliberately forget about doing any of these practices — concentrative meditation, vipassana meditation, and sensing, looking, and listening — for the rest of our Tucson III conference. You're going to be plunged into such a hyper-intellectual atmosphere, such a heavy orgy of concepts and ideas — which will be very valuable! I'm not putting them down, they will really be very valuable, but the odds are you won't be able to do our practices worth a damn, given the little bit of training we've had. If you try to do them, you'll probably mainly have failure experiences, and then you'll get into big, negative feedback loops: "Damn it! I thought I learned something and I can't do it, what's wrong with me, and blah, blah, blah!" It would probably be better to put practice off until after this particular conference and then when you get home, if you feel like doing some more with it — try it!

Regularity is usually helpful in learning things. So if you like one or both of the meditation practices we've learned, setting a regular time in your schedule to meditate is a good thing to do. You don't have to do marathon meditation sittings! If you do even ten minutes of quiet sitting a day, you are in the 99th percentile of people who are working on their inner development! If you do an hour a day, you are in the 99.9th percentile of people, because most people don't do anything to develop this kind of skill.

If you get real serious about following this meditative path, as I briefly said earlier, you should try to find a "coach," a teacher, in your hometown, someone you can practice with regularly and get some feedback from on how you're doing. If there are no meditation teachers in your home town (see the Appendix for sources of information), you might consider traveling to places that offer meditation retreats occasionally. Your classical meditation retreat will have sitting meditation most of the day, but there will usually be an interview time with the teacher so that you can check out how you're doing. As I said earlier, a lot of times a simple correction can make a big difference in how you practice. We get stuck in little dead ends that we've created on our own and don't recognize as such.

I've given you a fairly Buddhist slant on meditation, but don't worry about that. The actual procedure is designed to transcend labels. You don't have to become a "Buddhist" to learn the basic meditation procedures from teachers, even if they are called "Buddhists." If they are at all competent, they got the Buddha's message that the important thing is to help people understand their own minds by helping them learn and apply these tools, not putting a label of "Buddhist" or any other kind of "ist" on them. I don't call myself a "Buddhist." I can accurately call myself a "student of Buddhism" (as well as many other paths) because I'm trying to learn and understand, but that has never made me unwelcome in any meditation groups.

If you're interested in the self-remembering kind of practice, the only places I know of where it's practiced consistently is in various Gurdjieff groups around the country. I've always had ambivalence about recommending whether you should get in touch with any of them or not. G. I. Gurdjieff was a genius, but the people who claim to have carried on his work come, we could say, in a wide variety. Some of them are very aware and skillful individuals; some of them are people who believe they're very aware and skillful individuals, but have their limitations and neuroses. Some of them are very "far out," and some may be charlatans. I have heard of Gurdjieff groups that have definitely damaged people, others that have just made people feel bad about themselves — and others where people have learned really valuable mindfulness skills.

Note too that the main Gurdjieff teaching group in this country follows a tradition of not advertising. You have to be interested enough in that work and intelligent enough to find them. I'll leave that as an interesting puzzle.

Student: *Charley, I've worked in a Gurdjieff group, and the thing that works the best for me (you mentioned it earlier) is when you choose something that, every time you encounter it, it brings you back to self-remember. Like you talked about street signs, stop signs, doorknobs or thresholds, and to keep switching your reminder objects from time to time — it worked for me. It was very helpful.*

Yes, habituation is a deadly enemy on the mindfulness path, you're quite right. So if you can make up little exercises that build habits to remind you to sense look and listen — and then you actually make the little effort of will required so you actually sense, look, and listen — that's very helpful. But it's the conscious effort you make as a result of the habit reminding you that matters, not the habit itself! Again, be very careful to not confuse *thinking about* sensing, looking, and listening, which you can get in the habit of doing, from actually *doing* it! There are books of such exercises, too (see, e.g., (Orage 1965)) that you can find some places.

Oh, I should add this warning: *Getting involved with any spiritual growth group may be the best thing you've ever done in your life and/or it may be very dangerous and drive you to madness! Balance this with the fact that not getting in touch with any spiritual growth group may be the best thing you've done in your life and/or it may drive you to madness!*

Life is inherently dangerous — and wonderful! Whenever you do any meditative, self-remembering, or growth techniques in general, in a group setting, there is a "social energy" added to them which amplifies your ability to do them correctly — and which also tends to amplify your own and the group's limitations, flaws and neuroses.

In terms of the people who teach such groups, this social energy can amplify their effectiveness as teachers and/or also amplify their flaws. Students sometimes drive their teachers crazy if the teachers are not "perfect" (or at least accomplished and stable) to begin with. They're especially driven crazy by the expectation and projection of perfection from their students! You have a positive feedback loop that gets out of control.

So we have a little bit of time left. Any further questions or comments?

STUDENT: *Are you familiar with Centering Prayer?*

A little bit. I'm not going to say anything about it, though, because my familiarity is very small — but from the little bit I've read about it, it seems like a very useful technique.

STUDENT: *From what I've read it sounds like it's basically the same as insight meditation.*

It could be, but I can't really compare them. Every particular group and tradition adds a little something and takes away a little something from basic techniques for exploring and controlling the mind, based on their culture, the particular experiences and training of the founders, etcetera. Insofar as groups and organizations can remember that there is something essential they're going after, something deeper and more fundamental than the hallowed "sacred traditions" that tend to build up, it can work out okay. But whenever there is a group of human beings working together on almost anything, they'll develop their own sub-culture, based on satisfying ordinary social needs.

It's always a real and vital question as to whether any group has stayed close enough to essential realities to be able to train its members in them, or whether the essentials have gotten lost in protecting and preserving the sub-culture and the ordinary social needs which are fulfilled within that sub-culture. But from the little I know, Centering Prayer, done with real motivation to grow in compassion and wisdom, has got possibilities, yes. In general, the motivation you bring to any practice is vital, and may have a lot more to do with the outcome than the particular of the practice.

If you want to think of our day together and your future in terms of personal development, *the important thing for you to do is to find a path that has heart for you.* You might get involved in some growth path that's technically very proficient, but if it doesn't resonate deep inside somewhere, you're not going to do it with much dedication, so why bother? You've got to find a path that has heart for *you.* You may make mistakes along the way in finding that path. In fact, you're certain to make mistakes along the way, that's part of being human, so don't be too hard on yourself!

The world is full of teachers of meditation and related growth paths who have really important things they can teach us — and they are less than perfect. If you can treat them as *people*, who have something valuable to teach, yet who may have some flaws you may have to watch out for, great! But be careful when, psychologically, a teacher becomes a Teacher for you! I want to believe there are well-nigh perfect Teachers out there, but I think that too much of the time, when people think they have found their Teacher, its just a case of Freudian transference. The Magic Mommy or Magic Daddy archetype is being projected on to someone. That may make things apparently more effective at first, but the price to pay further down the line, when the teacher's imperfections are discovered and the student's positive transference ("She is a perfect Enlightened Being who knows my soul and bathes me in Perfect Love!") flips to a negative transference ("That bitch has been exploiting me all these years, my life has been wasted!") is very high.

It gets even more complicated when a teacher admonishes you to "surrender completely," but we don't have time to get off into the psychopathology of the spiritual path. In *Waking Up* (Tart 1988), I do have an appendix on choosing a developmental path and how to make it a little safer, through backing up from it once in a while to do an assessment. I would also strongly recommend Arthur Deikman's groundbreaking book *The Wrong Way Home* here (Deikman, 1990) as *essential* reading for anyone who might get involved with a "spiritual" study group of any sort. Indeed, the book has brilliant insights about the big "cult" we already belong to, ordinary society!

STUDENT: *Why are you here?*

Why am I here? Ah, the question of the ages! I will try to duck the deep aspect of that question, as I'm tired from teaching all day, but answer the simpler version of "Why am I here for the Tucson III Toward a Science of Consciousness conference?"

First, because I'm really interested in all sorts of aspects of consciousness, and I think all sorts of stuff that's going to be reported here is neat! Second, I'm also a kind of a technophile: I like these studies done with really complicated apparatus and techniques. I used to do research like that myself. Third, I think it's really important to have people from different disciplines talking to each other about the nature of consciousness.

Consciousness studies is much bigger than any one discipline. Any discipline can contribute something to understanding consciousness. The linguists, the philosophers, the neurophysiologists, the psychologists, the parapsychologists — all of them can contribute something, because consciousness is a multi-faceted reality. People in each field have a normal human tendency to try to claim consciousness as their territory and come up with the final word, of course. Each wants to capture mind and consciousness with a specific definition — in the terms of their specialty. I don't believe it can be done, as we discussed earlier, but everybody can add something.

Remember this old Zen saying, the finger pointing at the moon is not the moon? But pointing fingers can be real useful if it gets you to put your attention over there where you might see or experience something. That's real useful. Just don't stare at the finger. My cats have never been able to comprehend that: If I point at something and tell them to look, they stare at my finger. So I suppose we're slightly up on cats that way — at least some of the time!

STUDENT: *Coming back to the questions regarding psychedelic experiences. In my work, I've I taught mantra meditations, and I've done a tremendous amount of work in shamanism along the lines of Harner's core shamanism. He's described experiences with psychedelic drugs in various shamanic cultures and expanded on the use of shamanic techniques in various ways in our culture.*

Michael Harner's Core Shamanic work (Harner 1980) is excellent! I admire it greatly. Michael's an old friend, I've taken several of his workshops. I think it's great stuff, although I'm not particularly talented at it. But It's not the same as meditation.

STUDENT: *Are you saying that there is a very strong distinction between meditation and shamanic practice?*

Yes. A strong distinction. As a single example, when you're listening to a drum (external stimulus for changing state) and going on a shamanic journey (relative absorption in imagery usually related to a predetermined goal) you're not learning to focus your mind on one particular thing as in concentrative meditation, and you're not developing that focus and sensitivity that's involved in exploring the nature of the mind in a non-goal directed way, as in vipassana, insight meditation. Whether you ultimately end up at similar places in terms of long term change and enlightenment . . . well, ultimately I don't know, but you're certainly starting off with different techniques aimed at doing different kind of things.

What I really wish I knew, what a Western science of consciousness could and should develop, but we certainly don't have now, is specific and practically useful knowledge of which specific kind of developmental discipline is best for which particular kind of person. I have people come to me all the time and ask something like "I want to become more mature or spiritual, what should I do, what should I study?" I usually don't know how to give more than a pretty general answer involving too much "Try this, try that, see what happens."

One of my research dreams — and I put this strictly on an essential, empirical science level, since we don't have the adequately developed theory to do it — is that with the next hundred thousand or so people who go into various spiritual disciplines, we give them every psychological test we have. Then we follow them up every couple of years for the next thirty years. Thirty years later somebody comes in to our successors and asks a question like that and we say, "Take this test." The results of the empirically developed test are scored and we can advise a particular person something like "Well, whatever you do, don't do Zen! Your type of person has a 30 percent psychosis rate for Zen! Although 10 percent of your type feel they get enlightened, do you think, 1 in 3 odds of psychosis are worth the big risk? I don't know. However, with Sufi work for your type, 70 percent express satisfaction, the psychosis rate is only 2 percent." We might give the exact opposite advice for the next inquirer who is a different type of person.

I'd love to be able to give that kind of differential advice. What is a well-nigh perfect growth/development technique for one person may be a waste of time for a second person and a way to go nuts for a third person. By and large we simply don't know how to advise people very specifically on these matters. And I'm afraid that statement too often includes the teachers of various spiritual traditions. The teachers in most of those traditions tend to teach you the way they were taught. That works out very well for some people, but not for others.

As I've mentioned earlier, I'm very impressed with the work Shinzen Young is doing. He's not only putting meditation into a context Westerners can understand, he's also developing new teaching methods which, insofar I understand them, will make the process of learning to be a skilled meditator far more efficient than the traditional Eastern model. I'm following his work with great excitement. I usually go on a week-long meditation retreat with him once a year. I had to miss this the last couple of years, and I really miss the retreat and learning experience. As one example of the innovations he's working on, he's got a computer-based, expert-system type meditation "coach" now! Shinzen says it's not much, just a crude prototype, just a Mark I version, but I think it's fantastic! It's given me some of the best meditation teaching I've ever gotten.

This system is based on his extensive personal experience with many meditation techniques and outcomes, and his experience with the feedback he gets from people he's taught. The computer program asks you questions about what you experience in response to various meditation exercises, then makes suggestions on what to do, based on Shinzen's and his students' experience, then checks out your responses to those, etc. Shinzen feels this is just a first approximation to the inherent logic of teaching meditation. But I'm amazed at how effective it is for a first try. As it develops, we'll get an individual trainer model for meditation teaching instead of, "This is the way I learned from my Teacher who learned it from her Teacher and on and on through the centuries, so do it this way!"

But that's the future for most of us, and we're trying to learn to stay closer to the here-and-now, today. So if you want to get good at meditation, plan on going to meditation teaching sessions and retreats with a teacher or teachers you feel comfortable with, who inspire you and give you effective advice. There are lots of retreats and teaching centers around the country — this information is in Appendix Two. Ways to contact Shinzen will be in there — there are many other excellent meditation teachers, of course, people I've personally studied with, like James Baraz, Jack Kornfield, Sogyal Rinpoche, etc. I've mentioned Shinzen a lot today because I think Shinzen is an excellent teacher, and his style is especially appropriate for scientifically inclined people like us.

I do think there is a certain urgency for people in our society to learn meditation, and to learn to meditate with an efficient method. I look around at the world and see it run by a bunch of people who are really living in samsara, in illusion, in waking dreams, and increasing their own useless suffering and, as a result of their mindless and deluded behavior, increasing our useless suffering too as a result. There is a Sufi teaching story asking, "What's the best form of government for a mental institution? A republic? Communism? Democracy? A monarchy? Socialism?" The answer is that it doesn't matter which form the government takes, the people running the government will all be crazy, so whatever form of government they have, they're still going to screw up. The best form of government starts by getting people more sane. Then whatever particular form they use is going to be used in a much more sensible and kind manner.

I've just summarized my political philosophy in a nutshell, I guess. I believe in samsara! I know, from far too much personal experience, that I can be so spaced out and so out of touch with reality that I do all sorts of stupid and cruel things, yet I'm supposed to be a person who is intelligent, practical and in touch! If it's that bad for me, I hate to think of it on a large scale.

STUDENT: *More definitions.*

More definitions?

STUDENT: *One more. How would you define soul?*

How would I define soul? Oh, in terms of the "hard problem" that the philosophers at this conference will be talking about?

STUDENT: *Oh, never mind.*

Oh! That's good. That's good. Did you hear that? The answer to defining soul is "Never mind!" Yes, I like that!

"Soul," to me, is a word that says there is something in a certain direction that we ought to learn more about. The word is a finger pointing. Although it tends to be pointing a little like this (*CTT waves hand irregularly over a ninety degree arc.*) But at least there is a general direction. I can't "define" soul: come on now!

STUDENT: *During the break, I got up and was walking around, and I noticed that I felt that all my senses were functioning more sharply. Colors were brighter, lines were sharper, the breeze in the patio caressed me and carried subtle hints of interesting smells. It was neat!*

All your senses can be improved with mindfulness. It really is an "art museum" around here *if you're here.* It all depends on us. I used to walk home from work after my car pool dropped me off, and on the days I remembered to self-remember, I noticed that they'd added something new to the neighborhood every time! Quite amazing what they did for me! When did they put that elegant chimney on that house? What interesting texture on that garage wall! Look at the neat design in the concrete of the sidewalk! When did those tiny flowers start blooming?

STUDENT: *Are there any other teachers trying to make improvements in the teaching of spiritual techniques? You mentioned the one.*

Yes, I've mentioned Shinzen Young is making improvements in the techniques. His ideas are the ones I'm most excited about, and they are so far and above everything else I can think of offhand that I don't know who else to mention. This just demonstrates my narrowness of course, it doesn't mean that other teachers aren't experimenting and making improvements.

STUDENT: *Virtual reality. Could virtual reality techniques be used to improve the teaching of meditation?*

I don't know, it hasn't been tried, although I have had a lot of ideas on how virtual reality techniques could be used for psychological and spiritual growth and exploration (Tart 1991) (Tart 1993). Let me give you an example of the kind of improvements Shinzen Young is making.

STUDENT: *Shinzen Young is Japanese?*

No, he's an American, born in Los Angeles. Shinzen is the name he took when he became a Buddhist monk, and still keeps that as his teaching name, even though he stopped using the traditional external trappings of a Theravadin or Zen Buddhist monk years ago. He found it interfered with the effectiveness of his teaching Americans. If you wear funny clothes, like a monk's robe, and shave your head, it means you're very different from me, so I don't have to take you too seriously. Young is his real last name.

Years ago Shinzen was a graduate student in the most prominent graduate program in Buddhist studies in the United States, at the University of Wisconsin, and he was going to write his dissertation on meditation practices. He got this (unfortunately quite unscholarly) idea that perhaps he really ought to spend a little time learning meditation in a culture where people actually meditated, instead of just reading books about meditation! So he thought he would ordain as a monk for a while in Japan. "For a while" seems funny to us Westerners, but it's common in Buddhist countries for men to be monks for limited periods, and then go back to ordinary life. He had already learned both Japanese and Chinese as a teenager and spoke both languages fluently, as well as his undergraduate major at UCLA being oriental languages. His linguistic skills are formidable! For someone who's into meditation, who can transcend thought, he's so damned intellectual and smart it makes me a little jealous!

So Shinzen went to Japan and ordained as a Buddhist monk in the little-known Shingon sect of Japanese Buddhism, which is a lot like Tibetan Buddhism, with elaborate meditative practices. Then he continued his training in other branches of Buddhism. He was a monk or student in many Asian Buddhist traditions for many years, and never made it back to graduate school — the reality he's discovered was so much more interesting than clever words about the reality!

There is a fascinating video Shinzen produced as an introduction to meditation, "The Retreat," which also has historical footage of the Shingon monastery on Mt. Koya in Japan, where he had his initial training. (The video can be ordered from VSI, the Vipassana Support Institute, whose address is in Appendix One.)

Eventually he decided he would like to teach in the West, and came back. He thought at great length about how he could adapt what he'd learned in the East for the West. At first he taught in the traditional way that he had been taught. Then he thought about and studied the history of Buddhism. Buddhism originated in India, and then got transmitted to various other Asian cultures. In some cultures it got transmitted wholesale. When it went into Tibet, for instance, it basically took over from the earlier shamanistic religion, and while you can find elements of that earlier Bon tradition in Tibetan Buddhism, it's basically the Vajrayana Buddhism that came from India. But when Buddhism went into China, it came into a very sophisticated and old civilization, so it couldn't just come in wholesale, There were a lot of deliberate adaptations way back then as to how to redo Buddhism so it would "make sense" to sophisticated Chinese. Ditto for Japan.

Shinzen saw a clear parallel between Buddhism going into China and into the modern West, in both cases coming into a very sophisticated culture. He believed you can't remake Westerners into Tibetans or Indians or something like that. So how do you adapt Buddhist language and teaching methods in a way that makes sense for today's Western culture?

As an example, remember the little equation,

$$S = P \times R$$

Suffering = Pain multiplied by Resistance, that we discussed earlier for explaining the relationship between psychological resistance, suffering and pain? That's one of Shinzen's adaptations of Buddhist concepts, and a lot of Westerners, seeing that, have said, "Oh yes, that makes sense," because many of us think mathematically.

As another example, he's explained certain meditational focus techniques to me as not watching the phenomenon *per se* as your focus, but observing the *change* in the phenomenon — mathematically speaking you are observing the first derivative of the phenomenon. That made clear to me what had been confusing for a long time before.

For some people, that kind of explanation doesn't make "sense," of course. A derivative of phenomena? But for people with some mathematical background, that way of putting it communicates something quite clearly.

As another example of Shinzen's adaptations, he has done a lot of work on the idea and practice of giving people a "personal coach" or a "personal trainer" instead of having a meditation teacher. To reach people effectively, it helps enormously if you fit in with their culture — even if eventually we all have to transcend the limitations of our culture. Having a "meditation teacher" is weird by our culture's standards, creating a barrier, but having a "personal coach" or a "personal trainer" is Western and high status!

I expect big things here. I expect someday to be able to routinely call up a computer-based artificial intelligence meditation coach to get much of my basic meditation training. That will save the time of the really skilled teachers for the sophisticated stuff.

One final example, one that sounds simple by Western standards, but I suspect it will be revolutionary in increasing the effectiveness of meditation training. Eastern cultures that are big on meditation also believe in reincarnation and karma, karma referring to a law of cause and effect that goes from one lifetime to another, as well as operating within one lifetime. Karma means that you will eventually reap the rewards and sufferings of your good and bad actions — even if "eventually" involves a delay of many lifetimes. So in the East, if you've come around and want some meditation instruction, there is a tendency to think it was your good karma to have that desire to improve yourself. But if you don't stick around very long, don't learn to mediate, well, it's your bad karma not to stick around very long. Maybe you'll be back in another eight or ten lifetimes. Shinzen saw this as a culture-specific attitude.

When you teach meditation in Western cultures, it's been Shinzen's experience, and that of a lot of other Western meditation teachers now, that, of the people who come, almost all will definitely experience something very worthwhile, in even basic meditation training, and they will that say they want to stick with this. They want to make meditation a regular part of their lives. If you check back a year later, however, you're lucky if five percent of them are still doing any kind of regular meditation. There is no Western cultural support to keep meditation practice going.

Now because of the attitude in the East that such fallings away are a result of your karma, traditional Eastern teachers don't worry much about things like that. The other ninety-five percent will come back when the time is right, when their karma, the accumulated consequences and dispositional factors of many lifetimes, is right. If you think about this in Western terms, though, it's very different. Suppose you start a university and you have a ninety-five percent dropout rate? We expect a little more from an educational institution! So one of the simple things Shinzen has done that has made a big difference for a lot of people, is that during your initial meditation training, some older meditation student, someone who has been around for a while, is assigned to you as your "meditation buddy." Not that your meditation buddy is a "Teacher," not that they're all that "advanced," but your buddy is somebody you can call up once in a while and ask a question, or who'll call you once in a while and simply ask, "How's it going?" Well, the rate of people who stick with meditation practice goes way up that way, when you have a little bit of social support! Other vipassana teachers I know, like James Baraz, are doing similar things.

This lack of social support in our culture for meditation and mindfulness is part of the reason why I advised that when you leave our workshop tonight, you might as well stop this stuff for the rest of the Tucson III conference. I don't think there are going to be any moments of silence over in the main hall or any emphasis on mindfulness, but there is going to be a lot of intellectual stuff! It's going to get us thoughtaholics very drunk! And it's good stuff, but it's not conducive to meditation, so why stick a bunch of failure experiences on ourselves right away? But then later, after the conference is over . . .

So, it's that time. It's been a real interesting day. As you know, fellow addicts, I am an intellectual junkie. I love to talk, and I like to see people get excited and bounce intellectual ideas about and all that — but I also really like to see people being more attentive. I've seen a lot of that today! That's very rewarding in a very different, a very fundamental kind of way.

So at this juncture I will thank you for coming. I've had a great day, and I give you my best wishes that what you've learned today develops into something that will be really important and useful, both for you individually and, perhaps, in helping us move towards a science of consciousness.

Thank you for coming!

Notes

Chapter 1:

1. See Appendix 2 for information on The Archives of Scientists' Transcendent Experiences (TASTE) (http://psychology.ucdavis.edu/tart/taste/) or (www.issc-taste.org).

Chapter 3:

1. I expect to produce one or more tapes of guided meditation practice soon, and they should be available through the site www.paradigm-sys.com/cttart/ in early 2001.

2. Note added in press: I have been doing more detailed comparisons of hypnosis and meditation and should have a detailed paper on it available on my www.paradigm-sys.com/cttart/ site in 2001.

3. Since the workshop I've been quite honored by having *Altered States of Consciousness* selected as one of the hundred most important psychology books of the twentieth century by *Common Boundary* magazine! Although the book is officially out of print, autographed copies are still available through my web archives, www.paradigm-sys.com/cttart/.

4. Information about the Institute of Transpersonal Psychology program is available from them by mail at 744 San Antonio Road, Palo Alto, CA 94303 or from their web site, www.itp.edu.

APPENDIX I

Sources of Further
Information and Training

Learning and Practicing Vipassana Meditation

A subscription to the periodical *Inquiring Mind*, PO Box 9999, North Berkeley Station, Berkeley CA 94709 will give regular listings of vipassana retreats and seminars in the US and Canada. Subscription is free, but an occasional donation to help defray costs is appreciated — and needed! There are many excellent vipassana teachers in the US now.

The Insight Meditation Society, 1230 Pleasant St., Barre, MA 01005, (978) 355-4378, www.dharma.org, is the East Coast center for vipassana meditation and can also provide information of retreats around the US.

Spirit Rock Meditation Center, PO Box 169, Woodacre, CA 94973, (415) 488-0170, www.spiritrock.org/index.html, is the West Coast center for vipassana meditation and can also provide information on retreats around the US.

The Barre Center for Buddhist Studies, 149 Lockwood Road, Barre, MA 01005, (978) 355-2347, http://dharma.org/bcbs.htm provides more scholarly education on Buddhist meditation.

The **Vipassana Support Institute** organizes and supports Shinzen Young's workshops and retreats, has his schedule, and sells tapes of his talks. VSI can be contacted at 4070 Albright, Los Angeles, CA 90066 (310) 915-1943, vsi@gte.net. Shinzen's web site is www.shinzen.org.

How-to Books on Vipassana

Here are some excellent books on meditative practices, on the how to side of things.

Dhirivamsa (1984). *The Way of Non-Attachment: The Practice of Insight Meditation.* Wellingborough, Northamptonshire, England: Turnstone Press.

Goldstein, J. (1987). *The Experience of Insight: A Simple and Direct Guide to Buddhist Meditation.* Boston: Shambhala.

Goldstein, J. (1994). *Insight Meditation: The Practice of Freedom.* Boston: Shambhala.

Goldstein, J., and J. Kornfield (1987). *Seeking the Heart of Wisdom: The Path of Insight Meditation.* Boston: Shambhala.

Gunaratana, V. H. (1993). *Mindfulness in Plain English.* Boston, Wisdom.

Kabat-Zinn, J. (1990). *Full Catastrophe Living: Using the Wisdom of Your Body and Mind to Face Stress, Pain and Illness.* New York: Dell.

Kabat-Zinn, J. (1994). *Wherever You Go There You Are: Mindfulness Meditation in Everyday Life.* New York: Hyperion.

Kornfield, J. (1993). *A Path With Heart: A Guide Through the Perils and Promises of Spiritual Life.* New York: Bantam.

LeShan, L. (1975). *How to Meditate: A Guide to Self-Discovery.* New York: Bantam.

Salzberg, S. (1995). *Loving-Kindness: The Revolutionary Art of Happiness.* Boston: Shambhala.

Sogyal Rinpoche (1992). *The Tibetan Book of Living and Dying.* San Francisco: HarperCollins.

Sole-Leris, A. (1986). *Tranquility and Insight: An Introduction to the Oldest Form of Buddhist Meditation.* Boston: Shambhala

Books on Meditation Research

For those who want to look at the scientific research on meditative practices, the following summary books will get you started in the literature.

Murphy, M., Donovan, S. and Taylor, E. (1997). *The Physical and Psychological Effects of Meditation: A Review of Contemporary Research With a Comprehensive Bibliography, 1931-1996.* Sausalito, CA, Institute of Noetic Sciences.

Naranjo, C., and R. E. Ornstein (1971). *On the Psychology of Meditation.* New York: Viking Press.

Shapiro, D., and Walsh, R. (1984). *Meditation: Classic and Contemporary Perspectives.* New York: Aldine.

West, M. A. (1987). *The Psychology of Meditation.* Oxford: Clarendon Press.

APPENDIX II

The Archives of Scientists' Transcendent Experiences

Readers of this book, whether working professionally as scientists or not, will find this web site, The Archives of Scientists' Transcendent Experiences (TASTE) (http://psychology.ucdavis. edu/tart/taste/ or www.issc-taste.org) of interest.

Scientists today occupy a social role like high priests, telling us what is and isn't real, and consequently what is and isn't important: no one wants to give their energy to an illusion that isn't real. Unfortunately, the dominant materialistic/reductionistic psychosocial climate of contemporary science (scientism, which we've discussed earlier), suppresses and actively rejects both having and sharing certain essential experiences, experiences roughly described by such words as "transcendent," "transpersonal," "spiritual," or "psychic." As a psychologist, it is clear to me that such rejection of part of our human nature harms and distorts both scientists' and laypersons' spiritual potential. This rejection occurs because while science is idealistic in aim, it has too often widely degenerated, in practice, into the dogmatic, materialistic belief system sociologists have called scientism. This is a manifestation of Gurdjieff's waking sleep or what we have discussed as samsara or maya. Spiritual experience and wisdom, no matter how important, is (often vehemently) dismissed as "nothing but" illusory brain actions in an inherently material, and ultimately meaningless, universe.

I can best illustrate this sad situation by presenting a teaching exercise I use for helping students in some of my classes and workshops to become more aware of how much *all of us*, as members of modern culture, have consciously (and even more importantly, unconsciously) accepted and automatized much of scientism's beliefs. In the context of a "belief experiment" exercise, I have them recite aloud, in a group, the following "Western Creed." (Dashes in the text indicate slight reading pauses — to allow implications to sink in. The reader may want to try reading it aloud to get some of the impact.) Almost everyone who does this exercise, even people who believe they are strongly spiritually oriented, are horrified to see how much they implicitly accept and are affected by the following tenets:

THE WESTERN CREED
A Belief Exercise
by Charles T. Tart

I BELIEVE — in the material universe — as the only and ultimate reality — a universe controlled by fixed physical laws — and blind chance.

I AFFIRM — that the universe has no creator — no objective purpose — and no objective meaning or destiny.

I MAINTAIN — that all ideas about God or gods — enlightened beings — prophets and saviors — or other non-physical beings or forces — are superstitions and delusions. — Life and consciousness are totally identical to physical processes — and arose from chance interactions of blind physical forces. — Like the rest of life — *my* life — and *my* consciousness — have no objective purpose — meaning — or destiny.

I BELIEVE — that all judgments, values, and moralities — whether my own or others — are subjective — arising solely from biological determinants — personal history — and chance. — Free will is an illusion. — Therefore the most rational values I can personally live by — must be based on the knowledge that for me — what pleases me is Good — what pains me is Bad. — Those who please me or help me avoid pain — are my friends — those who pain me or keep me from my pleasure — are my enemies. — Rationality requires that friends and enemies — be used in ways that maximize my pleasure — and minimize my pain.

I AFFIRM — that churches have no real use other than social support — that there are no objective sins to commit or be forgiven for — that there is no divine retribution for sin — or reward for virtue — Virtue for me is getting what I want — without being caught and punished by others.

I MAINTAIN — that the death of the body — is the death of the mind. — There is no afterlife — and all hope of such is nonsense.

I am not trying to demonize scientists here: as you know, I am proud to be a scientist, and I like and respect almost all of my colleagues. Scientists are people, with, I believe, a full spiritual nature and potential. As scientists, however, we face especially strong obstacles to consciously even recognizing, much less developing, our own spirituality because of the pervasiveness and power of scientism in the scientific community. Scientists know they would almost certainly be ridiculed and rejected, and quite possibly have their careers hampered or even ruined, if they spoke publicly of their spiritual beliefs and experiences. So most scientists not only do not tell others about this aspect of their lives, they suppress it in themselves.

Perversely, because scientists do not speak of spiritual things, it further reinforces the implicit norms that scientists should not speak of such things, further reinforcing the belief that spiritual experiences don't happen to "real" scientists or to rational people. Thus we have a vicious cycle that is hard to break out of.

For better or worse, however, scientists function, as mentioned above, as high priests in our society, telling the rest of us what is real (and so, worthwhile) and what is unreal and nonsensical (and so, not worthwhile and "crazy"). If most scientists were genuinely open minded and knew the current limitations of science as well as its uses, and did not confuse essential science with paradigmatic science and scientism, this situation might not be too bad. But since too many scientists are mindlessly conditioned in the narrow grip of scientism, this high priest function is a social disaster. My own and others' research has convinced me that it is psychologically and spiritually pathological to deny any real aspect of the human spirit. This widespread denial of the spiritual by scientists causes a great deal of unnecessary suffering, not only among scientists themselves but in anyone who's had any sort of spiritual experience, i.e., in modern culture generally.

The Archives of Scientists' Transcendent Experiences (TASTE) project has four major scientific and humanitarian goals. My aim is to change this restricted and pathological climate through the operation of a World Wide Web site which allows scientists to share their personal, transcendent experiences in a safe, anonymous, but quality controlled space that almost all scientists, as well as the public, have ready access to. Specifically TASTE:

(1) allows individual psychological and spiritual growth in the contributing scientists by providing a safe means of expression of vital experiences;

(2) leads toward a more transpersonally/spiritually receptive climate in the scientific professions which, in turn, benefits our world culture at large;

(3) provides research data on transcendent experiences in a highly articulate and conscientious population, scientists, likely leading to books and articles about the findings, which will further help change the social climate to one more knowledgeable of and friendly to transcendent experiences;

(4) facilitates the development of a full spectrum science of consciousness by providing both data and support for the study of transcendent experiences.

The TASTE web site is basically an online journal, a psychologically safe and familiar format for scientists. A reader may go to the *Current Edition* page, which contains the dozen most recent experiences posted, and/or may go to the *Archives*, which is an accumulation of all posted experiences. Submissions to the TASTE site are limited to bona fide scientists, but anyone may read and use the material.

Reading the accounts on TASTE while sensing, looking, and listening will be especially interesting.

The Archives of Scientists' Transcendent Experiences (TASTE) web site URL is http://psychology.ucdavis.edu/tart/taste/ or www.issc-taste.org.

Appendix III

References

Aserinsky, E. K., N. (1953). Regularly occurring periods of eye motility and concomitant phenomena during sleep. *Science 118*: 273-274.

Bannister, R. (1987). *Sociology and Scientism: The American Quest for Objectivity.* Chapel Hill: University of North Carolina Press.

Blofeld, J. (1977). *Mantras: Sacred Words of Power.* London, Allan & Unwin.

Broughton, R. (1991). *Parapsychology: The Controversial Science.* New York, Ballantine.

Castaneda, C. (1968). *The Teachings of don Juan: A Yaqui Way of Knowledge.* Berkeley, California: University of California Press.

Chalmers, D. (1996). Facing up to the problems of consciousness. In *Toward a Science of Consciousness: The First Tucson Discussions and Debates.* Hameroff, S., Kaszniak, A. & Scott, A. (Eds.), Cambridge, MA, MIT Press: 5-28.

Deikman, A. (1990). *The Wrong Way Home: Uncovering the Patterns of Cult Behavior in American Society.* Boston: Beacon.

de Ropp, R. (1968). *The Master Game: Beyond the Drug Experience.* New York, Dell.

Dhirivamsa (1984). *The Way of Non-Attachment: The Practice of Insight Meditation.* Wellingborough, Northamptonshire, England: Turnstone Press.

Fromm, E., Brown D., Hurt S., Oberlander J, Boxer A., and Pfeifer, G. (1981). The phenomena and characteristics of self-hypnosis. *International Journal of Clinical and Experimental Hypnosis, 29,* 189-246.

Gates, B. (1989). Reflections on the suttas. *Inquiring Mind, 6* (Summer): 4.

Goldstein, J. (1987). *The Experience of Insight: A Simple and Direct Guide to Buddhist Meditation.* Boston: Shambhala.

Goldstein, J. (1994). *Insight Meditation: The Practice of Freedom.* Boston: Shambhala.

Goldstein, J., and J. Kornfield (1987). *Seeking the Heart of Wisdom: The Path of Insight Meditation.* Boston: Shambhala.

Gunaratana, V. H. (1993). *Mindfulness in Plain English.* Boston, Wisdom.

Harner, M. (1980). *The Way of the Shaman: A Guide to Power and Healing.* San Francisco: Harper & Row.

Hess, D. (1992). Disciplining heterodoxy, circumventing discipline: Parapsychology, anthropologically. *Knowledge and Society: The Anthropology of Science and Technology,* 9: 223-252.

Hess, D. (1993). *Science in the New Age: The Paranormal, Its Defenders and Debunkers, and the American Culture.* Madison, WI, University of Wisconsin Press.

Irwin, H. (1994). *An Introduction to Parapsychology.* Jefferson, North Carolina, McFarland.

Kabat-Zinn, J. (1990). *Full Catastrophe Living: Using the Wisdom of Your Body and Mind to Face Stress, Pain and Illness.* New York: Dell.

Kabat-Zinn, J. (1994). *Wherever You Go There You Are: Mindfulness Meditation in Everyday Life.* New York: Hyperion.

Kornfield, J. (1993). *A Path With Heart: A Guide Through the Perils and Promises of Spiritual Life.* New York: Bantam.

Kuhn, T. (1962). *The Structure of Scientific Revolutions.* Chicago: University of Chicago Press.

LeShan, L. (1975). *How to Meditate: A Guide to Self-Discovery.* New York: Bantam.

Malcolm, N. (1959). *Dreaming.* London: Routledge & Kegan Paul.

Martin, B. (1998). Strategies for dissenting scientists. *Journal of Scientific Exploration,* 12(4): 605-616.

Murphy, M., Donovan, S. & Taylor, E. (1997). *The Physical and Psychological Effects of Meditation: A Review of Contemporary Research With a Comprehensive Bibliography, 1931-1996*. Sausalito, CA: Institute of Noetic Sciences.

Naranjo, C., and R. E. Ornstein (1971). *On the Psychology of Meditation*. New York: Viking Press.

Orage, A. R. (1965). *Psychological Exercises and Essays*. London: Janus.

Orne, M. S., and Scheibe, K. (1964). The contribution of nondeprivation factors in the production of sensory deprivation effects: the psychology of the "panic button." *Journal of Abnormal Psychology*, 68: 3-12.

Radin, D. (1997). *The Conscious Universe: The Scientific Truth of Psychic Phenomena*. New York: HarperEdge.

Salzberg, S. (1995). *Loving-Kindness: The Revolutionary Art of Happiness*. Boston: Shambhala.

Schoek, H. and J. Wiggins (1960). *Scientism and Values*. Princeton, New Jersey: Van Nostrand.

Shapiro, F. (1995). *Eye movement desensitization and reprocessing: basic principles, protocols, and procedures*. New York, Guilford Press.

Sheldrake, R. (1988). *The Presence of the Past: Morphic Resonance and the Habits of Nature*. New York: Vintage Books.

Sogyal Rinpoche (1992). *The Tibetan Book of Living and Dying*. San Francisco: HarperCollins.

Sole-Leris, A. (1986). *Tranquility and Insight: An Introduction to the Oldest Form of Buddhist Meditation*. Boston: Shambhala

Tart, C. (1972). A psychologist's experience with transcendental meditation. *Journal of Transpersonal Psychology*, 3, 135-140.

Tart, C. (1972). States of consciousness and state-specific sciences. *Science, 176*: 1203-1210.

Tart, C. (1975). *States of Consciousness*. New York: E. P. Dutton.

Tart, C. (1986). *Waking Up: Overcoming the Obstacles to Human Potential*. Boston: New Science Library.

Tart, C. (1987). The world simulation process in waking and dreaming: A systems analysis of structure. *Journal of Mental Imagery* 11: 145-158.

Tart, C. (1991). Influence of previous psychedelic drug experiences on students of Tibetan Buddhism: A preliminary exploration. *Journal of Transpersonal Psychology*, 23, No. 2, 139-173.

Tart, C. (1991). Multiple personality, altered states and virtual reality: The world simulation process approach. *Dissociation, 3*, 222-233.

Tart, C. (1994). *Living the Mindful Life*. Boston: Shambhala.

Tart, C. (1995). Yes, we are Zombies, but we can become conscious. *Journal of Consciousness Studies*, 2, No. 4.

Tart, C. (1998). Investigating altered states of consciousness on their own terms: A proposal for the creation of state-specific sciences. *Ciencia e Cultura, Journal of the Brazilian Association for the Advancement of Science*, 50 (2/3): 103-116.

Tart, C. T. (1993). Mind embodied: Computer-generated virtual reality as a new, dualistic-interactive model for transpersonal psychology. In K. Rao (Ed.), *Cultivating Consciousness: Enhancing Human Potential, Wellness and Healing*. Westport, Connecticut: Praeger: 123-137.

Terkel, S. (1984). *The Good War: An Oral History of World War Two*. New York: Pantheon.

Wallace, R. K. (1970). Physiological effects of Transcendental meditation. *Science*, 167: 751-754.

Walsh, R., Goleman D., Kornfield J., Pensa C. and Shapiro, D. (1978). Meditation: Aspects of research and practice. *Journal of Transpersonal Psychology*, 10, 113-134.

Wellmuth, J. (1944). *The Nature and Origins of Scientism*. Milwaukee: Marquette University Press.

West, M. A. (1987). *The Psychology of Meditation*. Oxford: Clarendon Press.

INDEX

A

absorption, 134
access concentration, 103
addiction, 136
Adler, Alfred, 113
aggression, 16
agnosticism, 4
Aikido, 60, 61
aliveness, 119
Alpert, Richard, 186
altered states of consciousness.
  See ASCs
alternating attention, 130
archetypes, 172, 204
artists, 143
ASCs, 52, 94, 96, 97, 98, 99,
  174, 176, 177
ASCs, induction techniques,
  157
Aserinsky, Eugene, 168
assumptions, 95
asthma, 64
atheism, 4
attachment, 20, 21, 68

attention, 78
attraction, 69
audiolizing, 65
authenticity, 119
authoritarianism, 10
automatization, 85, 137, 143
aversion, 68, 69, 86

awakening, 108

B

Bannister, Robert, 5
Baraz, James, 208, 214
Barre Center for Buddhist
  Studies, 219
basic scientific attitude, 7
beauty, 137
Behaviorism, 27
belief, 39, 151, 154
belief vs. direct experience, 5, 7
bias, 16, 21, 22, 23, 29, 163,
  164, 165, 166, 167, 184
bliss versus joy, 56
Blofeld, John, 65
body, 58, 60, 61
Bon, 212
breath, 49, 73
breath as meditation object, 42
Broughton, Richard, 170
Buddha, 98, 109, 151, 154,
  155, 158, 179, 180
Buddha nature, 62
Buddhism, 21, 23, 28, 46, 58,
  59, 62, 93, 151, 154, 156,
  157, 158, 185, 200, 211, 212

C

Castaneda, Carlos, 179
Centering Prayer, 202, 203

psychology as introspective
science, 150
psychosis, 172
psychotherapy, 47
psychotomimetics, 182
purification, 158
purifying ordinary consciousness, 97
purpose, 52, 224

Q

quantum physics, 1
quantum physics and con-
sciousness, 170, 171
quieting, 32

R

Radin, Dean, 170, 229
Ram Das, 186
range of experiences, 178
rationalization, 18
reality, 224
reality contact, 13, 188
realms of existence, 58
reincarnation, 46, 213
religion, 3, 5, 6, 156, 174
resistance, 80, 82, 133, 212
retreats, 208
right brain functions, 78

S

Salzberg, Sharon, 220, 229
samadhi, 180
samsara, 46, 59, 106, 107, 109,
144, 208, 209, 223
Scheibe, Karl, 160, 161, 162,
229
schizophrenia, 52
Schoek, Helmut, 5, 229
science, 2, 3, 10, 11, 131, 149,
156, 165, 166
science vs. scientism, 5
science and religion, 1
science of consciousness, 27,
29, 32, 95, 105, 149, 150,
151, 154, 155, 163, 164, 165,

166, 167, 169, 205, 206, 226
science vs religion, 156
scientific study of consciousness, 13
scientism, 5, 6, 8, 9, 15, 223,
225
self observation, 109
self remembering, 131
self-hypnosis, 44, 45
self-observation, 103, 107, 112,
113, 114
self-remembering, 12, 17, 103,
107, 118, 119, 120, 123, 132,
137, 146, 186, 187, 198,
199, 201
sensing, looking, and listening,
123, 127, 131, 132, 133, 134,
135, 137, 138, 139, 141, 142,
144, 146, 165, 186, 188,
198, 199, 201
sensory deprivation, 159, 161,
163
shamanism, 184, 205, 206
Shapiro, Dean, 131, 221, 230
Shapiro, Frances, 229
Sheldrake, Rupert, 35, 229
Shingon, 211
shoulds, 42
sin, 225
skepticism, 10
skillful means, 9
sleepiness, 63, 64, 74
social energy, 202
Sogyal Rinpoche, 57, 64, 208,
220, 229
Sole-Leris, Amadeo, 220, 229
soul, 209
sound, 91
space between thoughts, 119
spaciousness, 118, 119
Spirit Rock Meditation Center,
219
spiritual inquiry, 6
spiritual seeker, 2
spirituality, 2
spirituality vs. religion, 5